WANT TO LIVE IN AMERICA?

YOUR PATHWAY TO LEGAL STATUS

JOE. K MUNGAI

WANT TO LIVE IN AMERICA?
YOUR PATHWAY TO LEGAL STATUS

Joe K. Mungai

Copyright 2019 © Joe K. Mungai

ISBN: 978-1-7339798-2-5

Joe K. Mungai
2150 James St # 5204 Coralville
IA 52241 USA
Ph. +1319-325-3225
Fax: +1319-338-1717
Email: contact@beinformedimmigrant.com
www.beinformedimmigrant.com

Facebook: https://fb.me/aninformedimmigrant
Tweeter: https://twitter.com/BeImmigrant

Published and distributed in the USA by:

BREMA GROUP ENTERPRISES LLC
P. O. Box 5204 Coralville IA 52241

Personal Knowledge Imparting Books or certain sections of the books are available at a special discount for bulk purchases by corporations, institution and other organizations. Contact the publisher at: contact@speakoutspeakup.life

TABLE OF CONTENTS

DEDICATION

I would like to dedicate this book to all the men and women who throughout the years have had the will and selflessness to share their knowledge of this subject to those eager to learn.

Their impact has been profound on me. It's their wisdom that you hear in these words.

I cannot even begin to express how grateful I am to their contribution and how greatly enriched I am by all the others who have walked the path before me and have made such a difference in my life. They all deserve recognition. I did my best to soak in all that I read and heard, and observed, and in turn, what I learned seeped into my thoughts and words.

The information you will find in these pages is what I've utilized and shared with countless others with great success.

I'm hoping that in some way, this book will make an equally big difference in your life through the content that I share.

FOREWORD

It is my great pleasure to write this foreword for Joseph Mungai's book. I was delighted when he asked me to write it. I have known Mr. Mungai professionally as a court certified interpreter for over many years now, and have had the opportunity to work with him on multiple cases. I cannot think of anyone more qualified to work with and support immigrant's efforts to attain stability, integration and realize their identity and citizenship in America than Mr. Mungai.

In my interactions with Mr. Mungai, he has always been dependable, respectful and compassionate. Each of these qualities is why he has been sought out for his services on multiple occasions.

Mr. Mungai is very knowledgeable about the difficulties within immigrant populations and, more importantly, also very knowledgeable about the many opportunities to strengthen the integration process for immigrants into the community as a whole. He is sincere in his desire to use his talents, gifts and experience to serve the greater community of immigrants and refugee families. I believe that the work that he is doing is a calling which he is uniquely qualified to answer.

His desire to expand his work within this population through this book will provide a much-needed resource guide to the immigrant community in America and beyond. He has my support and the support of many other professionals who have worked with him to ensure the success of this endeavor.

I am grateful that these resources are going to be available and accessible to those who need them most at this critical hour. May you be enriched as you read WANT TO LIVE IN AMERICA? YOUR PATHWAY TO LEGAL STATUS, and become better equipped to navigate our complicated immigration system.

Geneva L. Williams
Attorney at Law

PREFACE

"We have always believed it possible for men and women who start at the bottom to rise as far as the talent and energy allow. Neither race nor place of birth should affect their chances." – Robert F. Kennedy

I have realized that many immigrants in America and those intending to move there do not know where to find helpful resources, or how to use the resources available to them to improve their circumstances in life. The resources include helpful immigration information that can make a huge difference on the path to citizenship for immigrants. The aim of this book is to provide you with resources and information that is freely available and accessible to everyone, which you might have not been aware of, or maybe you did not know where to find it.

My intention is to encourage you and also to educate you so you become more aware of the resources and information that is available, and how you can use it for your success.

Certain assumptions about you, as an immigrant, have guided the content of this book.
1. You care about your success in the immigration process and you want to improve your abilities so as to develop needed skills to help you achieve your targets.
2. You want to know specific information that others have used successfully, which also immigration researchers have found to be effective.
3. You can figure things out for yourself. Once you are

presented with the gist of information, you can adopt it to your particular circumstances or reject it as inappropriate for you.

4. You are busy and have little time to search for information on immigrants' path to citizenship and other related topics. You want to be able to quickly find the information and ideas you need to improve your specific immigration situation (for those who wish to do further reading and research, each resource or article includes a source at the bottom).

Although each resource shared is designed to be read on its own merit, there is a certain amount of repetition and overlap of the information which I hope the reader will not find annoying or distracting. Furthermore, not all suggestions shared in this book are compatible to all the situations of an immigrant. But they represent a wide variety of helpful strategies from which you can select those that best address your needs.

Origin of Helpful Immigration Success Tips & Hacks for Immigrants in U.S.

There is a lot of useful information about immigration that is available. This book is an attempt to share immigration strategies, ideas and information that has been tried and tested. In preparing this book, I reviewed a lot of information and selected what seemed most helpful and worthwhile for helping immigrants towards attaining American identity and citizenship.

The information shared comes from a variety of sources:

1. Broad conversations with both immigrants and attorneys that I work with every day.

2. The resources shared by other attorneys and practitioners who provide immigration and immigrant-services related support all across the U.S. and beyond.

I have made every effort to credit every resource and article to the source. If any required acknowledgements have been omitted, it is unintentional. If notified, the publishers will be pleased to rectify any omission in future editions. In some cases, the ideas form the general lore and common practices, or they reached me without reference, while some evolved from my own experiences in the course of working with immigrants and providing services to them.

Finding Trusted Immigration Legal Service Providers

One of the reasons I credit the source apart from giving you more information to help you do your own research is because I'm interested in directing you the immigrant towards trusted immigration resources support and legal service providers. I don't have any partnership with the authors, organizations or resources whose source I give; but I have relied on the information they share and offer to immigrants because it's the most evidence-based information we have in this field.

I have guided many immigrants to find and locate trusted immigration legal service providers for several years now. This is important to me because I need to ensure that the confusion caused by current immigration debates and shifting laws does not allow notarios and other unauthorized practitioners of immigration law to take advantage of members of our communities.

Why You Should Read this Book

"Immigration is the American way. And Immigrants make the United States great." – CitizenPath

This book details the roadmap to the path of adopting American identity and citizenship. This is important because it opens the doors for you as an immigrant to integrate into the American society.

Why is Integration Important?

The successful integration of immigrants and their children into the American society has two main benefits:

1. It opens important avenues – jobs, higher education, legal services, social services and health care – just to name a few, that offer success and stability to immigrants.
2. It contributes to America's economic vitality and its vibrant and ever-changing culture.

How Integration Happens

Integration is a two-fold process: it happens because immigrants experience transformation once they arrive and interact with American systems, and also because native-born Americans also experience a transformation in response to immigration.

It's clear though, that the process of integration cannot happen without participation of immigrants and their descendants within major social institutions in America such as school or education systems, health institutions, labor market and business, as well as their social acceptance by other Americans.

In the course of my work in America, as a social worker, I have met immigrants from every walk of life; I have seen and appreciated their contribution to this country in many ways, especially protecting the United States through military service. This became very clear to me when I worked for the U.S. government through the department of veteran's affairs. I also see immigrants serving America in the health care industry, in the technology sector, transportation, farming and construction – just to name a few. This includes enriching every domain of American life through art, culture and language.

The relationship between immigrants and their host country is one that can be described as an exchange. By taking up and utilizing the opportunities that America has given them, immigrants have been able to better themselves and support their communities overseas. And the services that the immigrants offer, of course, benefit America and its people.

One thing that has made this exchange possible has been the process of integrating immigrants into America and incorporating them fully into the society. This phenomenon alone has nurtured and created this exchange that allows immigrants to give their best as a result of being embraced by their new society. The important thing to note here is that this process largely happens as a result of immigrants assuming American identity and citizenship which I call in this book legal status.

I see opportunities and barriers to integration of immigrants in the United States today as shaped by their status in America – which can either be legal, or illegal. At present, an immigrant legal status in America is one of the most important achievements one can ever get. It creates varying degrees of stability and opportunities, with potentially profound implications for positive integration. For both the American society and the immigrant's community, knowing the pathway to acquiring this legal status is of utmost importance. This is the subject of this book.

Your Feedback is Important

Kindly send your comments on the subjects and ideas presented in this book – what you found valuable and what you didn't find valuable. Let me know what you think and please, pass along good ideas and suggestions you would want to see shared in a future book. Send your suggestions to contact@beinformedim-migrant.com or visit our community page at www.beinformed-immigrant.com

DOJ Recognition and Accreditation

This kind of feedback will be helpful to me for my own improvement because my mission is to work with immigrants and help them address their most pertinent immigration issues. As part of my preparation for this work, I am in the process of completing my DOJ Recognition and Accreditation to provide immigration services directly as a legal service provider. This will allow me to help those immigrants in dire need to see some form of immigration relief that they are eligible for but which they might not be aware of.

INTRODUCTION

"We have a great dream. It started way back in 1776, and
God grant that America will be true to her dream."
– Martin Luther King, Jr.

Every immigrant in America likes a sense of belonging, which
is most notably quantified in the form of citizenship.

America was built by immigrant. This continues to be the
case even now. As a country, America has experienced
transformation through successive waves of migration from
almost every part of the world. This reality is widely recognized in the familiar image of the United States as a nation
of immigrants. Integration of immigrants into the American
society is then important, if these immigrants will continue to
build America like those who came before them.

Legal status remains the greatest obstacle to integration.
Therefore, knowing how to acquire legal status is paramount.

Legal status has varied over time in its consequences for
immigrant integration. Early in the country's history, little
attention was given to legal status. Non-citizens could even vote
in federal elections. The American Constitution did not forbid
non-citizens from voting in federal elections until the 1920s.

In recent times, however, the importance of legal status
has grown, as have the variety of different legal status that
immigrants can hold. And so, utilizing all legal avenues that
the U.S. offers to attain legal status should be a goal of every
immigrant living in the U.S. today.

We all know that despite the current anti-immigrants' wave, the U.S. continues to have one of the most generous immigration policies in the world, with its provisions for diversity program, asylum seekers, refugees, family reunification, and workers who bring scarce employment skills.

Integration Has Not Always Been a Smooth Process

What we see happening now is not new to those who are students of American history. Americans have sometimes failed to live up to ideals of full inclusion and equality of opportunities for immigrants. Many descendants of immigrants who are fully integrated into the American society today remember the success of their immigrant parents and grandparents. And they also remember the resistance they encountered before they were fully integrated.

This is why it's important to not give up and get off the path to American citizenship, or allow yourself to fall of the wagon, no matter what.

I want you to know that the immigration restrictions we are experiencing today were also experienced by past generations of immigrants at different times in the American history. And during those times, there were policies that were enacted just like now that limited the numbers of legal immigrants permitted from certain countries, and putting in place restrictions on immigrants across the United States' southern border, which set the stage for the rise in undocumented border crossers. This is exactly what America is experiencing right now.

In Pursuit of the American Dream

Most immigrants don't find a congruence between their experiences and the American dream – at least what they have heard about the American dream. What happened to the spirit and soul of the inscription on the statue of liberty: "Give me your tired, your poor, your huddled masses yearning to breathe free, the wretched refuse of your teeming shore."

Does America not represent the universal dream of escaping repression, that of starting over, living free, pursuing happiness, and building a successful life with your own resourcefulness and hard work – a dream shared by people of all races, religions, ethnicities, and national origins? Mary Kearney a licensed Immigration attorney boldly asks.

Yes, it does. That is the response that many people who still believe in the ideal that America holds and is made of, would say. Yes. We are. We do. We're still America – land of the free and home of the brave. They would say.

Mary Kearney further asserts: "The great majority of Americans strongly believe in the ideals of our country and will stand and fight for them. But meanwhile, our government's been taken over by a deranged minority of haters. They're fomenting, right here at home, a filthy, toxic brew of the very evils we came to America to get away from. Evils such as tyranny, oppression, discrimination, cruelty, exclusion, suppression of free speech and Religious persecution.

These true Americans who still believe in what America stands for would say, "We drafted our Constitution specifically to prevent these things. It's a robust, strong, sturdy Constitution. It's a good antidote to poison. It will neutralize these evils, eventually. But it's going to take time."

Staying True to the Wishes of our Founding Fathers

Like these true sons and daughters of America, I believe that if history is anything to go by or learn from, we will eventually get out of this mess. And although it might take time, all the wrong done will be undone in terms of the policies.

So, this is not time to be disappointed, or to give up the fight towards attaining citizenship. This is the best time to do what you need to do to move on to the next level on the pathway of American citizenship.

Many individuals and families are missing out on what is rightly theirs by not taking the right steps towards attaining legal status right away.

Taking Advantage of Immigration Benefits

Every day I interact with immigrants of different legal status who wait for several years before attaining lawful permanent resident (LPR) status. Also, a huge number of immigrants of lawful permanent residents become citizens after living in the United States for an extended period of time.

There are also immigrants under different legal status but who eventually adjust to LPR status after several years. This gives you a picture of the number of immigrants who live in the United States for decades without officially immigrating, which holds back the process of integration.

I bet a number of those impacted negatively by President Trump's policies never thought a thing like this would ever happen. And so, they had not taken up the opportunities or checked to see which type of immigration relief they were eligible for. Since they just went on with life without action that would eventually enable them to attain legal status, when these policies were introduced, it was too late to do what they could have done few years before.

One of the chapters in this book is titled **DO WHAT YOU CAN WHILE YOU CAN**. Another one is titled **DON'T WAIT TOO LONG TO END UP BECOMING A STATISTIC.** Check them out and see why I suggest them.

Legal Status Removes Significant Barriers for Immigrants
Legal status offers formal security and removes significant barriers that hinder immigrant integration. Because of existing laws that make it easy to shift to legal status, one would think that there is enough motivation to move forward, but as I have shared, that is not the case most of the time. Maybe this is as a result of lack of knowledge on how to go about it. Knowledge is power, that's why it's important to empower immigrants with the information provided in this book.

Remember, legal status touches on areas that are fundamental for integration in a variety of ways, across a wide range of activities, and with varying degrees of intensity. And so, legal status has become increasingly important for immigrants' integration into the American society. I have seen the negative effect arising from lack of legal status. I have witnessed the devastating impact on families, particularly on children, when parents don't have legal status. The children might be American citizens, but the parents remain in the shadows, sneaking their way around some of the legalese because they are afraid to come out in the open where they can access support and services that their kids are entitled to.

I want you to know that you are denying others, including your children, benefits they could be enjoying if you had taken advantage of immigration laws and the opportunities that are in front of you. You need to get up and take the right action on the pathway to citizenship.

My American Journey

My American journey started when I landed in America as a visitor and then changed my status to that of a student and became a freshman in the University right away.

It didn't take that long for me to realize that America is the hardest country to migrate to, but at the same time, I quickly learned what makes America great. I wanted to be part of that ideal of greatness. I wanted to be part of that shared commitment to an ideal, that all of us are created equal, and that all of us have the equal chance to make of our lives what we will. I believe that this is what makes America most alluring to many. This ideal was compelling enough for me to stay and go through the daunting immigration journey to make my citizenship and identity official.

This would mean years-long journey through the American immigration system, since each category of visa and status has different processing times which is significant and varies with each application. It was challenging to make the transition from visa, to legal resident alien status, to naturalized citizen, but a decade later the dream was realized.

High Level Clearance Job

Since then, I have held different jobs in America, including two important public service positions of employment with the state and U.S. federal government. The most recent role involved working directly with U.S. military men and women and veterans, a position that required periodical top-level clearance to fill it. The position allowed me to not only see the impact of federal government policies on people first hand, it also gave me an opportunity to advocate and fight for individuals and groups of people affected by those policies. This includes educating them about those policies and why they exist, and the vast resources available to everyone in America.

Navigating Immigration Journey

My immigration experiences prompt questions from friends and strangers alike. I readily offer help and also connect immigrants to those who have legal expertise. Some of the referrals have made a huge difference in the lives of many immigrants in regard to their cases.

I realized that expertise to navigate immigration systems is expensive, and information is woefully scarce. And even when the information is available, it is scattered all over, bit by bit, so you have to spend considerable amounts of time and energy not only to search for it, but also to piece it together.

I also realized that trying to find an immigration attorney is unnecessarily burdensome. Online searches yield hundreds of potential candidates to sift through, but then there is no easy way to tell, for example, who speaks a foreign language, or if they took payment plans. The struggle of finding accurate immigration information and credible legal services was the basis for forming **Be Informed Immigrant online platform (BII).** A central location that helps individuals and businesses find high quality immigration attorneys in America and beyond. It's a crucial step towards helping people realize the ideal of what makes America great.

Simpler Solution

BII is a platform that connects immigrants with a smaller, vetted network of experienced lawyers and also provides content written by these lawyers to tackle some thorny questions at no legal expense at all. The participants are able to get connected to an attorney and other providers by state or specialty, and by what language they speak.

Benefits and Responsibilities of Citizenship

Becoming a U.S. citizen opened unstoppable doors for me. I realized all the benefits and responsibilities that come along. My mission now is to help others by connecting them with the resources and services that will make their journey easier and simpler.

Becoming a U.S. citizen allows you to have a voice in how the nation is governed since you are able to vote at many levels of leadership. You become eligible for Federal jobs. You also, become eligible for certain kinds of scholarships and grants. And, as a naturalized U.S. citizen, you can help a number of family members become U.S. citizens by sponsoring them. This allows you to start the immigration process for many of them.

PART ONE

COMING
TO AMERICA

CHAPTER 1

AN IMMIGRANT'S PERSPECTIVE

"I'm troubled by the current immigration debate. When my family came to America from England during the war, people said, "You are welcome here. What can we do to help?" I am a beneficiary of the American people's generosity, and I hope we can have comprehensive immigration legislation that allows this country to continue to be enriched by those who were not born here." – Madeleine Albright

Why Immigrants Come to America

There are several reasons that explain why immigrants come to America, but the predominant one is to make a better life for themselves and their children. This includes their communities back home.

As Catholic social teaching (CST) asserts, "People have the right to migrate to sustain their lives and the lives of their families."

In some cases, migration is necessitated by extraordinary circumstances, such as war or an epidemic. Joseph and his wife Mary were forced to flee – taking their son, Jesus, to Egypt, to avoid Herod's wrath back in Bethlehem.

In some cases, the same circumstances of war or epidemic

prevent the immigrants from safely returning home.

Needless to say, there are plenty of immigrants who move away from home in search of success and a better life. They are propelled by ambition, hard work and sacrifice, and a strong belief in America as a land of opportunity. Research has shown that immigrants are actually more likely to believe in the American dream than the native-born. Five years ago, almost seventy percent of immigrant parents said their children will prosper relative to themselves, compared to only fifty percent of native-born parents.

What Immigrants' Experiences Have Been with the Current Climate

As Arjun Rao, an Indian born immigrant observes, "There is a lot of hubbub around immigration into the United States at the moment." This is because of the slew of immigration orders and laws that have caused fear, doubt and uncertainty and have been struck into the hearts of immigrants.

It's a very tough time right now for immigrants all across the U.S. We have witnessed, read and heard of lives that have been turned upside down. Husbands, wives, and kids are being separated from each other. Others can't get back home from abroad. Mary Kearney notes that, "people are stuck in places they don't want to be. Orderly business planning for inter-national immigrant entrepreneurs has becomes a bad joke." Immigrants have to deal with this now in America, in addition to multitude of concerns that involve leaving behind families thousands of miles away.

We figured that immigration would get harder after the election, right? But we didn't know it would get this bad, this fast. We didn't know to what extent the dignity of the immigrants would be disregarded.

Once again, am reminded of another Catholic social teaching (CST) of embracing every person's human dignity and recognizing the rights of immigrants. These teachings which ought to be upheld and practiced by every true church that regards itself as Christ's representative on the face of the earth reminds us that:

We are our sisters' and brothers' keeper, wherever they may be. And loving our neighbors has a global dimension in a shrinking world. As followers of Jesus Christ, we know the dignity and worth of every person is at the core of the Gospel message. And this is not dependent upon immigration status or nationality. Jesus' message in the Gospel of Matthew says that the Kingdom of Heaven would be open to those who, when He was a stranger, welcomed Him (Math 25:35).

These teachings lead us to promote and defend the rights and dignity of our neighbors who benefit from Temporary Protected Status (TPS) and all immigrants who fear for their safety at the thought of returning to their country of origin.

What Immigrants Now Wonder About America
Most immigrants are now wondering whether this is the same

promised land of opportunities that we once knew. They are asking, what happens if America does not take strong and constructive steps in the right direction? Because this might as well cause it to lose the edge it commands on the world stage. Most of us believe that immigration reforms will help the best and brightest doctors, engineers, entertainers and entrepreneurs stay in the U.S. It will also help us stay true to our founding fathers' wishes.

As a country, we have to remember that family stability and unification are the foundation of society. And so, it's important to create Immigration reforms that keep the family unit together as opposed to what we are witnessing now.

We are reminded that how we organize our society – in economics, politics, law and policy – directly affects human dignity and the capacity of individuals to grow in the community (CST).

Unique Historical Influence of Fundamentalists in America
One most confusing aspect of America is that despites its enviable success, and its coveted position in the world as a beacon of hope, it allows a very small group of fundamentalists to continue influencing its policies and politics by acting out of fear and bigotry. This is what has created some animosity towards a section of immigrants residing in America right now. And although majority of immigrants are not aware of it, this has been a historical fact. We see earlier waves of immigrants facing racism and homophobic assaults. The current admin-

istration seems to be tapping into this dark history, which is causing it to bash immigrants instead of doing the opposite.

If you check American history, you'll find that there has always been some worry that immigrants and their children do not share the same social values as the native-born, and that after their arrival in America, the immigrants will not learn English, and so the dominance of English as the main language in the United States will be under threat. This is according to members of this small fundamentalist group.

This belief receives greater force when an illegal immigrant commits a horrible crime. Such crime perpetuates call for *a wall, to keep the criminals out.* This fear makes the small group of fundamentalists argue that immigrants are responsible for the increase of crime in America.

This group which comprises a portion of professing members of Christian faith expresses discomfort about the introduction of new and unfamiliar religions that immigrants might introduce when they settle in America. These fears are expressed by a minority of Americans, but they drive public discourse about immigration time and again.

The results of the actions of this small group of people create what has been called "a flaw in democracy," which is on show right now. In this set-up, as we are told, "People are too ignorant and removed to keep politicians in check." And so, we are reminded that, "when the U.S. implodes, it will be the fault of the small group of the people."

In December of 2018, Francis Wilkinson on *Bloomberg* pointed out that President Trump's bashing of immigrants happened at a time when Gallup recorded a new high of 75 percent of Americans saying that they believe that immigration is a "good thing." This in essence means that majority of Americans favor positive immigration reforms instead of polices that are made out of fear and bigotry.

PART TWO

LET THE EXPERTS SPEAK

CHAPTER 2

ADVICE FOR THOSE ASPIRING TO BECOME INTERNATIONAL STUDENTS

"In life, your success depends on what you do with the knowledge that is readily available." – Joe Mungai

10 Steps to Get a U.S. Student Visa: Full Application Guide

Most of the following information is from Prep-scholar Platform (See Prepscholar.com)

Each year, many international students apply to U.S. schools in order to study full-time in the U.S. But to attend school in the States, you need more than just good grades — you need a U.S. student visa. Unfortunately, the process for obtaining a visa can be complicated, which is why I'm educating you by sharing this knowledge with you.

In this guide, we'll go over the basics of visas and how to get a student visa to the U.S. We'll also give you a handful of tips and resources you can use to ensure your visa application process proceeds smoothly.

What Is a U.S. Student Visa? Do You Need One?

In order to legally attend school in the US, all international applicants — that is, those without U.S. citizenship or permanent residence — must first obtain a U.S. student visa. This international student visa allows you to reside temporarily in the U.S. in order to attend an approved school, language program, or academic exchange program.

Your student visa ends once you complete your program. At that time, you must depart the U.S. (However, you may later return to the U.S. as a tourist or on another visa, such as a work visa.)

There are three types of U.S. student visa:

F-1 visa: This visa is for high school or college/university (including language program) study in the U.S., applying to both undergraduate and graduate students.

M-1 visa: This visa is for non-academic or vocational study in the U.S. Such programs are usually short term and career focused. For example, you could attend a culinary school or a medical training program.

J-1 visa: This visa is for exchange visitors, including study-abroad students, scholars, interns, and au pairs.

Generally speaking, international students who wish to study full-time in an undergraduate or graduate program will need an F-1 visa. By contrast, if you're interested in studying abroad for only a semester or two at a U.S. institution (and want to receive credits that go toward your home institution), you'll need to apply for a J-1 visa.

When Should You Apply for a US Student Visa?

You may only apply for a student visa after you've applied for and been accepted to an SEVP-approved school. (SEVP stands for the Student Exchange and Visitor Program. All US schools that enroll F-1 and/or M-1 students must be certified by this program). Once you've secured admission to the school you wish to attend, you can begin the visa application process.

Note that you must receive your visa before your program start date. While you can receive your US student visa up to 120 days before your program start date, you may not travel to the US on this visa until 30 days before your start date.

US Student Visa Application Checklist

Before we explain how to apply for a student visa, let's briefly go over the specific items you should have in order.

#1: Passport

Every international student must possess a valid passport issued by his or her home country. This passport must also be valid until at least six months beyond the end date of your program in the U.S. So any passport that will expire during your stay in the U.S. or shortly after your program ends may not be used. Rather, you'll need to apply for a new passport and use that one instead.

Passport procedures and costs vary by country. Check your country's government website for details on obtaining or renewing a passport.

#2: Passport-Style Photograph

As part of your application, you must submit a recent (within the past six months) passport-style photograph. This will be your visa photograph, which you will later upload and submit with your online visa application.

The U.S. visas website offers specific instructions on how to take and upload a visa photograph, as well as examples of acceptable and unacceptable photographs. Be aware that as of November 2016, glasses are no longer allowed in visa photographs.

#3: Money
Finally, you'll need to have a decent sum of money on hand so that you can pay the various visa-related fees. We'll discuss in more detail what these fees are and how to pay them later. But as a brief overview, here are the required fees for a U.S. student visa:

I-901 SEVIS fee: This fee is 200 USD for F-1/M-1 students and 180 USD for J-1 students (or 35 USD for those entering short-term J-1 programs). All applicants must pay this fee.

Visa application fee: This fee is 160 USD. All applicants must pay this fee.

Visa issuance fee (if required): This fee is only required for applicants of certain nationalities. You can see whether you are required to pay a visa issuance fee by going to the U.S. visas website. Also, remember to always confirm the fees as this information was current at the time this book was being compiled.

How to Get a Student Visa: 10-Step Guide
Now that you understand the basic items you'll need to have

ready, let's walk through how to apply for a student visa, one step at a time.

NOTE: The application process for an F-1 visa is identical to that for an M-1 visa and similar to that for a J-1 visa. As a result, the visa process described below may be used for all three types of U.S. student visas. If you have any questions about your visa type or how to apply for one, consult the U.S. visas website.

Step 1: Apply and Get Accepted to a U.S. School

The first step is to apply (and eventually gain admission) to a U.S. school. Most full-time undergraduate and graduate programs in the U.S. require applications to be submitted by December or January each year. Schools typically send out admission notifications around March and April.

As I mentioned previously, the schools you apply to must be approved by SEVP. To find an SEVP-approved school or to confirm that the schools you've chosen are in fact certified by SEVP, use the SEVP school search tool.

J-1 students will most likely apply for exchange programs through their home institutions. You may also look for designated sponsor organizations online at the official J-1 visa website.

Step 2: Receive Form I-20 or DS-2019 from Your School

Once admitted to a school, you'll receive one of two forms: F-1 and M-1 students will receive Form I-20 (Certificate of Eligibility for Nonimmigrant Student Status), and J-1 students will receive Form DS-2019 (Certificate of Eligibility for Exchange Visitor (J-1) Status).

Your school will mail the appropriate form to you. On your form will be your SEVIS ID, your school's address, and other critical information concerning your program. You will need this form for your visa interview (we explain the interview process more in step 8) and to pay certain fees (which we discuss next in step 3).

Step 3: Pay the I-901 SEVIS Fee

Once you receive your I-20 or DS-2019 form from your school, go online and pay the I-901 SEVIS fee. Once again, this fee is 200 USD for F-1/M-1 students and 180 USD for J-1 students. (Those participating in short-term J-1 visa programs will pay only 35 USD).

Most students (except those from Cameroon, Gambia, Ghana, Kenya, or Nigeria) can pay this fee online by credit card. Note that the I-901 SEVIS fee is separate from your visa application fee (which we explain more in step 7).

Once you've paid this fee, print out your confirmation page, as you'll need to bring it to your visa interview.

Step 4: Find Your Nearest US Embassy or Consulate

You must apply for your international student visa through your nearest US embassy or consulate (ideally, in the city or region in which you live). You can search for U.S. embassies and consulates online through the U.S. Department of State.

Be aware that U.S. student visa processes may differ slightly depending on the embassy through which you apply. This means that at some embassies, you may need to submit additional documentation with your visa application. For more details on what you'll need to submit, go to your embassy's official website or contact your embassy directly.

Step 5: Complete Form DS-160 Online

Next, complete the Online Nonimmigrant Visa Application, also known as Form DS-160. To successfully fill out this form, be sure you have the following items on hand:

Your passport.

A visa photograph (to upload).

Form I-20 or DS-2019 (remember, which form you receive depends on whether you are an F-1/M-1 or J-1 student).

In addition, you may need to supply:

A travel itinerary (if you've already made travel plans to the US).

The dates of your last five visits to the U.S. (if applicable) and/or evidence of your international travel history within the past five years.

A resume or CV.

Additional information depending on your purpose for travel.

On this application, you will also select the U.S. embassy at which you intend to interview for your visa.

Note that you must fill out the entire form in English, except when asked to input your full name in your native alphabet. Translations are available on the form for those who have difficulty understanding the English instructions. If you have any additional questions about how to fill out this form, go to the official DS-160 FAQ page.

Once you've completed this form and submitted it online, print out your confirmation page to bring to your visa interview.

Step 6: Schedule Your Visa Interview

After you've submitted Form DS-160, contact your nearest U.S. embassy or consulate (ideally, the one you input on your online application) to schedule your visa interview.

Wait times for interviews vary depending on the embassy. Go to the U.S. visas website to see the wait times for your embassy.

Step 7: Pay Your Visa Application Fee

Next, pay the 160 USD application fee. This fee is the same price regardless of your country of origin and where you apply.

Note that when you pay this fee will vary depending on your embassy. Although many embassies require applicants to pay the application fee before their interviews, not all do. Your embassy should instruct you as to when and how you'll need to pay your visa application fee. If your embassy requires you to pay this fee before your interview, be sure to bring your receipt as proof of payment to your interview.

Step 8: Attend Your Visa Interview

The last big step in the visa process is the interview. This interview will be the deciding factor as to whether you will receive a U.S. student visa or not.

Before attending your interview, gather the following items and information:

Your passport.

One copy of your visa photograph (this may be required by certain embassies, particularly if you were unable to upload your visa photograph to your online visa application)

Your printed DS-160 confirmation page.

Your printed I-901 SEVIS fee confirmation page.

Your visa application fee payment receipt (this is only required if you paid the application fee before your interview).

Form I-20 for F-1/M-1 students, or Form DS-2019 for J-1 students (make sure to bring the original form — not a copy)!

Your particular embassy may require additional forms and documentation, such as:

Official transcripts from colleges/universities you've attended.

Diplomas/degrees from high schools/colleges/universities you've attended.

Standardized test scores (if required by your US school).

Proof of sufficient funds.

Proof of your intent to depart the US at the end of your program.

You will undergo a security check and provide digital, ink-free fingerprints, usually right after you arrive at your interview.

During the interview, you will be asked a range of questions in

English. These questions will mostly focus on why you want to study at the school you've selected and what you intend to do after the program finishes. It is important to clearly state that you do not intend to remain in the U.S. once you complete your program. Websites such as International Student and Happy Schools offer extensive lists of sample questions you may be asked during your interview.

If your interview is successful, your embassy will then inform you when and how it will return your passport (with your new visa) to you. (To get your visa, you must leave your passport with your embassy).

Step 9: Pay the Visa Issuance Fee (If Required)
Some students must pay a visa issuance fee once they have been approved for a US student visa. Whether this fee is required or not depends on your nationality and your country's reciprocity agreement with the US. The US visas website offers a tool you can use to see whether you must pay a visa issuance fee.

Step 10: Receive Your Visa
Once you've completed all of the steps above and have received approval for an international student visa to the U.S., your embassy will return your passport to you with your new visa in it. Note that some embassies will require you to come in person to pick it up, whereas others will mail it directly back to you.

Visa processing times will vary depending on your embassy. You can get an estimate as to how long your visa will take to process by going to the U.S. visas website.

What If You Are Denied a U.S. Student Visa?

According to the U.S. visas website, most applications for U.S. visas are approved. That said, in rare cases, you may be denied an international student visa. This typically only happens when you fail to fulfill a certain requirement before or during your interview.

Here are some examples of problems likely to make you ineligible for a U.S. student visa:

You do not provide proof of sufficient funds. This is said to be one of the main reasons students are often denied student visas to the U.S. Although you aren't necessarily expected to have enough money to last you the entire duration of your program, you should possess proof of sufficient funds (in liquid assets) for at least one academic year.

You do not provide proof of your intent to leave the U.S. once your program ends. The U.S. government needs to ensure that you will not (intentionally or accidentally) overstay your visa. Therefore, you must provide adequate proof of your intent to return to your home country once you finish your program.

You do not pass the security check (good conduct records). Though this may be obvious, committing certain crimes can make you ineligible for a U.S. visa.

You do not bring all required items to your interview. Failure to bring all required items, such as your passport, receipts, and official visa-related documents, may result in a visa rejection.

You fail to show up to your interview. If you are late to your interview or simply fail to show up, your application for a visa may be rejected.

You apply for a U.S. student visa too late. Applying for your visa with too little time before your program starts will most likely make you ineligible for a student visa. This is mainly because your visa won't become available to you until after your program-start date.

This list highlights some of the many reasons international students are denied U.S. visas. If your application for a student visa is rejected, your embassy will tell you why. Unfortunately, you cannot get your money back in the case of a rejection. Moreover, embassies will not reevaluate visa applications, so if you are rejected, you must repeat the process above in order to reapply for a student visa.

In the end, visa rejections are not common. As long as you do everything you need to do and follow the steps we've given you, you should have no problem obtaining a U.S. student visa!

3 Tips for Ensuring a Smooth Visa Application Process
You now know how to get a student visa — but how can you make sure you won't face any problems along the way? Follow our three tips below to ensure that your visa application process proceeds without hassle.

#1: Start Early
Applying for your visa with too little time before your program starts will most likely result in a visa rejection, so try to apply for

a student visa as soon as you are accepted and have received Form I-20 or Form DS-2019 from your school.

If you are applying to multiple U.S. schools, I recommend waiting to apply for a visa until you have received admission notifications from all of your schools, or until you have received an acceptance to your top-choice school. Doing this allows you to weigh your options and choose the best school for you.

#2: Don't Buy a Plane Ticket Until You Have Your Visa

Although it's a good idea to start the student visa application process early, it's best not to buy any plane tickets until after you've received your visa since there's no guarantee that your application will be approved.

If you purchase a plane ticket ahead of time and are then rejected for a U.S. student visa, you will most likely not receive a full refund for your airfare. (Refund policies vary depending on the airline, but usually you cannot get a full refund if you cancel more than 24 hours after booking a flight).

#3: Contact Your Embassy if You Have Questions

The visa application process described above is the general process for securing an F-1, M-1, or J-1 international student visa to the US. That said, you may find that your visa process differs slightly from the steps described above. Usually, this is due to differences in how U.S. embassies choose to handle or process certain information.

As a result, always direct any questions or concerns you have about the visa process to your closest embassy. Your embassy is hands down the best resource for questions about fees, the interview, and other visa-related matters.

Source: Prepscholar. Compiled by Hannah Muniz

Additional Resources for International Students

If you want clarification or extra guidance on certain aspects of the U.S. visa application process, here are a few official resources we recommend using:

U.S. Visas Official Website: This website is an official government website that covers everything you need to know about student visas, including how to apply for them, what kinds of visa policies there are, etc. Some excellent pages to look at if you have questions are the U.S. visa FAQ and the visa fees pages.

Study in the States: This official government website is run by the U.S. Department of Homeland Security. By clicking on the "Students" tab at the top of the page, you'll get tons of information on how to apply for a student visa, how to prepare for your arrival, and how to maintain your F-1 or M-1 visa status. You can also get the rundown of all of the major student forms you'll need to fill out for your U.S. student visa.

Education USA: This government website run by the U.S. Department of State helps international students navigate possible U.S. schools, funding options, the visa application process, and more.

J-1 Visa Exchange Visitor Program: The J-1 visa can be a little confusing for students, as it applies to non-students as well. Use this website to learn more about what the J-1 visa entails and how you can apply for one.

CHAPTER 3

QUALIFYING FOR US VISITOR VISA OR B-2 TOURIST VISA

"Make your life experience work for you, for a change." – Joe Mungai

I found this article, which was compiled by Siam Legal law firm International, helpful. See what you can learn from it.

Also known as a U.S. Visitor Visa, a B-2 Visa is a non-immigrant visa that is issued to qualified applicants who intend to go to the U.S. on a temporary basis for medical treatment or simply for leisure purposes. It specifies the purpose of the travel as well as the length of stay of the holder. Such type of visa can also be issued for the following purposes, namely; to visit the family in the U.S., to attend a special event, family functions or ceremonies, or purely for tourism. However, it cannot be granted for business purposes because a U.S. Business Visa is the appropriate visa for that purpose. A person granted with a B-2 Visa is allowed to stay in the United States for a period of 6 months or less and may apply for an extension of stay which application is subject to approval. It must be stamped/placed in the traveler's passport.

In order to qualify for a B-2 Visa, the applicant must be able to prove that he/she qualifies under the Immigration and Nationality Act. Under the U.S. Immigration Law, when a person applies for a Visitor Visa, the presumption that the applicant intends to be an immigrant arises. So in order to refute such presumption, the applicant must be able to establish the fact that he/she has a residence in the country where he/she came from and that he/she has no plans of abandoning the same. He/she must also be able to prove that his/her stay is only on a temporary basis and is not for good. Owning a house in the home country and having been able to travel to different countries are some of the facts that are taken into consideration for an easy obtainment of a B-2 Visa.

It is important to note a holder of a B-2 Visa is not allowed to work in the United States. The I-94 card will tell the holder thereof the length of stay in the U.S. One who intends to stay in the United States for good cannot rely on the B-2 Visa since this type of visa is specially designed only for the fulfillment of a specified predetermined purpose. Once the number of days of stay as stated in the I-94 card have already elapsed, the B-2 visa holder will be ordered to leave the U.S. otherwise, he/she will be facing a 3-year or a 10-year ban to enter the US.

Source: Siam Legal law firm International

How to Increase Your Chances of Obtaining a US Visa
I found the information below helpful because it's based on both personal experience in obtaining a visa in the United States, and the experience of those people who have used my consultation.

Most of these pointers were shared by Alexey Gavrilyuk of CaliforniaTrip.ru.

The process of obtaining a visa in the United States actually consists of two stages – the preparation of the questionnaire and an interview. And the very fact of obtaining a visa is strongly influenced by objective factors that cannot be changed, and subjective factors that can be corrected in their favor.

Here is Alex's perspective:

I do not care why you need a U.S. visa, and talk about popular tourist visas of category B1 / B2, which many use as a step to stay in America forever. The purpose of the trip is exclusively yours but remember that obtaining a cherished visa depends not only on the correctness of filling out the questionnaire, but also on whether the visa officer believes your history.

It often happens that people do not believe the true stories, and vice versa, stories made up for the purpose of immigration work out.

Objective Factors Affecting the Receipt of a US Visa

Briefly about what cannot be fixed in the visa application form:

Relatives in the USA. I do not advise hiding the presence of relatives living in the USA - it will only be worse. The same applies to cases when parents or one of the parents live in the States.

Age and gender. It is clear that for a lonely girl or a guy of 20-25 years, it is extremely difficult to get a visa, but it's worth a try, since there are many other subjective and objective factors. If the other factors are against you - work, income, travel history, you will either have to risk money and go to the embassy in spite of everything or wait a bit and during this time you will have to change something for your own good.

All other questions of the questionnaire either do not affect the receipt of a visa, or they can be treated creatively.

Subjective Factors Affecting the Receipt of a Visa in the United States

I call them subjective, because some data, as well as its history, can be presented in different ways. Accordingly, the result will also be different. You will either receive a US visa or NOT.

Job. It is rightly considered an important factor of binding to the motherland. A good high paying job increases your chances and vice versa. Work does not have to be the so-called "official," that is, with a record in the workbook. She just has to be. Of course, there are many verification programs, but not everything is so straightforward.

Work is considered to be any source of income, even informal. The main thing is that it is legal, I hope this is understandable and true.

The questionnaire should indicate the main source of income. You can conduct business training, you can rent an apartment for rent or do needlework - knit items for sale. This is all your work.

What should be the income for a visa in the United States?

There is no direct connection, but income should allow travel to the States for tourist purposes. For example, to travel to New York on 10 days, you need no less than $ 1200 - $ 1500.

Legend or Purpose of a Trip to the USA

You can tell the truth that you are going to a second cousin for her granddaughter's wedding, and DO NOT get a visa, or you can write a story about going to visit the auction of agricultural equipment in New Mexico, although you are actually going to work as a truck driver. These are two real stories. In the first case, the person did not get a visa, but the future truck driver already plows Idaho's expanses on a large, brilliant truck. I do not urge to lie - but simply cite real examples.

So, the legend is the main subjective factor. Legend should be linked to your life in your homeland. What did I mean by that? If you are an IT person, you may well go to the conference on new digital technologies, but an invitation is necessary. But you can go to an exhibition dedicated to mobile communications, without an invitation, for example, in order to get acquainted with future partners.

Are you a young lady who makes a living by renting apart-ments? Then you can safely say that you are going to New York for Christmas sales, shopping is a great reason to fly to New York. If you are a successful entrepreneur (this should be seen from the questionnaire), then you may be going to Las Vegas, and an avid tourist who has several countries in Southeast Asia in his possession can say what he is going to see. US national parks.

The History of Your Previous Trips

It really matters when getting a tourist visa and if the goal is pure tourism. If you, besides Turkey, did not go anywhere, you shouldn't compose that you are going to travel for tourist purposes in America - most likely, no one will believe you, even if this is true.

If there is no travel history, higher chances are those who are going to a seminar-conference-exhibition or to visit friends. If the travel history is rich - feel free to say that you are going to travel around America, for example, California - a state rich in sights.

Increase of the chances by using bus tours and a couple of Schengens does not work, it is a waste of time and money. Better change the purpose of the trip in accordance with your activities.

If you want to increase the chances of getting a visa in the United States in this way, then for a year or two, travel to distant countries, then go to the embassy again. This is a reliable, but long and costly path that is not suitable for everyone.

English
This is a negative factor for obtaining a visa in the United States, but not always. If you are just going to travel, then you need English within the school curriculum and you can indicate in the questionnaire that you do not know it.

But if you are going to look for partners at the exhibition or are going to refresher courses - English is needed and their knowledge will be accurately verified, just the visa officer will switch to English.

Behavior at the Visa Interview
Your goal of obtaining a visa and a trip to the United States may be true, or it may not be true, which is no secret. Visa officers

also know this. But they often believe fictional stories and DO NOT believe the truth.

Simple Tips

I risk being captain-obvious, but experience shows that everyone who is denied a visa in the United States makes similar mistakes. So, read again, even if you all know what you think.

Answer confidently, all your intentions must be combined with your lifestyle.

Answer short and accessible, no one likes complicated multi-pass stories.

Answer sincerely but make it clear that the refusal of a visa will not be a huge tragedy for you.

Do not be afraid and do not worry. Stinging and trembling in the voice - a sign that you will NOT get a visa. Just calmly answer the questions, without anguish and unnecessary showing. Smile, but do not abuse. Do not try to please the officer - it is useless.

Remember and believe for yourself what you are going to do at the interview. Key questions may relate to the purpose of your trip, your work at home and your income. The interview lasts no more than 3-4 minutes.

Dress simple, like in the office or in the movies. So as not to distract the visa officer from work. I think you understand me.

Plan your goal of traveling to the USA correctly, formulate the right occupation and source of income, correctly evaluate your travel history and your chances of getting a visa will increase. Checked on yourself.

The most important thing

At the visa interview, the consultant who helped you with the documents will NOT be there, you will not look at the Internet for hints either. Rely only on yourself - and everything will turn out.

Good luck to all!

Additional ways to increase the chance of getting a US tourist visa which I modified for this subject.
Gladsy Gozon, a Content Writer for a Travel Group - UK put this together and posted on Quora.com

Here is Gladsy's perspective:
I think that the best way to increase the chances of getting your U.S. visa approved will depend on the way your interview goes aside from your documents.

Just so you know, it is very important that you know how to respond to the Consul's questions correctly. While it matters that your documents can prove that you will go back to your home country, you still need to have conviction during the interview proper. It would only last for a few minutes and trust me, you can't make a second first impression, so you have to nail it!

Here are some tips on **How To Handle Tourist Visa Rejections (And What You Can Do to Avoid It)** from Kach Howe. These are the tips I kept in mind all throughout my visa application interview and I nailed it! I got a 10-year multiple entry visa)!

1) Complete all the required documents. Almost all the

embassies require the same set of documents for visa application so make sure you have everything ready and don't miss out even a single one.

2) Prove your deep-rootedness/deep ties in the home country as much as you can. This can be proved by providing additional supporting documents such as your School details and School Enrollment records if you are a student, your Employment records if you're an employee, Business Registration if you're an entrepreneur.

   You may also include Car Registration, Land/Condominium Titles, Proof of Investment, Contract of Lease in your favor, etc. if you have any.

3) Collect passport stamps, not enemies. If it's your first time traveling and you're going to a far country like those in the US or Europe, chances are the Consul Officials will doubt you, your financial capacity, as well as your intention to return.

   So, I suggest that you should travel around closer countries first and collect passport stamps. You can always cross countries that are near your home country. You can also cross borders from your home country to countries further away to gather more travel history. Not only will you get to travel and enjoy, you'll also get a lot of passport stamps and higher chances of approval for your next visa.

4) "Dress on how you want to be addressed." Some embassies require an interview and remember, "You never get a second chance to make a second impression." So, go ahead and put on your decent clothes - slacks/pants, closed shoes,

and a polo shirt/long sleeve.

Look what you say you are - if you're a student then you should dress like one (not necessarily in your school uniform but if you have class on the same day then why not?), if you're a businessman then wear something semi-formal.

5) Provide only authentic documents. Don't you dare give them a fake document because once they find out, you'll be denied your visa outright or worse, you could get black-listed. Yikes!

6) Have a "2-minute elevator pitch" but briefly, truthfully, and concisely. This is very important. Most of the questions asked by the consuls are answerable by a maximum of five words. Questions usually asked are: "What kind of work do you have?" "Who are your traveling with?" "What's the purpose of your travel?" "Who's going to pay for it?" etc. Please do prepare a very quick answer for each of this question.

7) Be confident. Lack of confidence can be seen in your overall aura - your eyes, your voice, your hands, the way you stand, and even the way you walk. So make sure this doesn't show. It's normal to be nervous but you have to relax! These people don't bite and are just there doing their jobs).

Good luck!

CHAPTER 4

HOW TO BECOME A U.S. CITIZEN THROUGH NATURALIZATION

"I received a letter just before I left office from a man. I don't know why he chose to write it, but I'm glad he did. He wrote that you can go to live in France, but you can't become a Frenchman. You can go to live in Germany or Italy, but you can't become a German, an Italian. He went through Turkey, Greece, Japan and other countries. But he said anyone, from any corner of the world, can come to live in the United States and become an American." – Ronald Reagan

For immigrants in the United States, becoming a citizen is often a long and stressful process. Once achieved, the rewards include rights and privileges such as voting, traveling using a U.S. passport, bringing family members permanently to this country, sponsoring citizenship for children born abroad, and obtaining government benefits.

The legal process is known as citizenship through naturalization. To get started, immigrants must meet six key requirements, according to the U.S. Citizenship and Immigration Services (USCIS).

Here's what you have to do.

Requirements for Naturalization
- An applicant must be at least eighteen years old at the time of filing.
- Live in the United States as a permanent legal resident for five continuous years, or three if he or she got a green card through a U.S. citizen spouse.
- Show physical presence in the United States for at least thirty months during the last five years, or eighteen months if married to an American.
- Show good moral character. This means a clean criminal record for the previous five years, and not submitting false information as part of any immigration form or procedure. (A person with an aggravated felony is ineligible for naturalization).
- Be able to read, write and speak basic English, and show knowledge of U.S. history and government.
- Be willing to support and defend the United States and the U.S. Constitution.

Applying for U.S. Citizenship
To apply for naturalization, legal residents must submit, by mail or online, Form N-400, Application for Naturalization. The form must be properly filled in, strictly following these USCIS instructions.

The form must be submitted along with $725 fee payment, which includes $85 for the biometric services. USCIS accepts money orders, credit cards, personal and bank checks payable to the U.S. Department of Homeland Security. Remember to check USCIS website to confirm the fees as this information was current at the time this book was being compiled.

The application also has to include all evidence and supporting documentation listed. Do not send original documents unless specifically required.

Some of these documents are:
- Two passport-style photos.
- Copy of the permanent resident card, known as a green card.
- Copy of current legal marital status document.
- Documents for armed forces members or their spouses, such as certification of military or naval service using Form N-426.

BIOMETRIC SERVICES APPOINTMENT

Once the application has been submitted, USCIS will schedule an appointment for the biometric services – to take finger-prints, photo and signature. The information is later sent to law enforcement agencies for criminal and security checks.

The procedure, in a local USCIS Application Support Center, normally takes fifteen to twenty minutes. It is important to show up on time for the appointment.

Applicants must bring with them the following:
- Notification of the appointment, Form I-797C.
- Valid photo IDs such as passport, green card or driver's license.
- Any other documented specifically requested in the notifi-cation.

Naturalization Interview and Exam

One of the key requirements for obtaining U.S. citizenship is the much feared naturalization test, in which immigrants must prove they can read, write and speak basic English, and have essential knowledge of U.S. history and government. There are some exemptions to the English language requirements.

USCIS publishes study guide materials for the civics portion of the test – which encompasses 100 questions and answers – and for the language section. There are plenty of other free online resources. Immigrants can also watch a video about the interview and test process.

Applicants must correctly answer six of ten questions to pass the civics test. In the English portion, they must correctly read and write one out of three sentences. The ability to speak English is determined by the USCIS officer conducting the interview on Form N-400.

This interview consists of questions about the applicants' background and his or her N-400, which is signed at that time. Some original documents ought to be brought to the interview, including:

- Green card.
- Valid driver's license or other state-issued identification.
- Passport and other travel documents.
- Evidence of current legal marital status.
- Evidence that previous marriages, if any, have legally ended.
- IRS income tax returns.
- List of trips outside the United States, with departure and return dates, during the last five years.

- Criminal record, if any, such as arrest reports, court dispositions, sentencing reports and evidence of probation completion.

Naturalization Ceremony

Once USCIS approves the Application for Naturalization, the agency will coordinate the date to take the Oath of Allegiance in a public ceremony. It is preferable not to postpone it.

Immigrants first turn in their green cards, then swear loyalty to the Constitution and at the end receive their Naturalization Certificates, which is official proof of U.S. citizenship. Authorities recommend that new citizens also obtain U.S. passports through the Department of State Bureau of Consular Affairs.

Afterward, new citizens are encouraged to register to vote and update their Social Security records at their nearest Social Security Administration office.

Citizenship carries with it benefits and obligations, such as:
- The right to U.S. government protection.
- The right to vote.
- The right to work.
- The right to live permanently in the United States.
- The obligation to obey all federal, state and local laws.
- The obligation to report income to the IRS.
- The obligation to register with the military Selective Service, for males aged eighteen to twenty five.

(Source: Marta Cravlotto Oliver & DANIEL SHOER ROTH. Miami Herald 2019)

CHAPTER 5

HOW TO GET A GREEN CARD

"Immigrant families have integrated themselves into our communities, establishing deep roots. Whenever they have settled, they have made lasting contributions to the economic vitality and diversity of our communities and our nation. Our economy depends on these hard-working, taxpaying workers. They have assisted America in its economic boom." – Senator Edward M. Kennedy

The American Dream that continues to attract immigrants to the United States starts with a valuable document: the permanent residence card, or green card.

The green card provides three important rights to immigrants who have it: to live permanently in the United States, to work at any legal work and enjoy the protection of all local, state and federal U.S. laws.

The following guide, based on official information from the U.S. Citizenship and Immigration Services (USCIS) and other government resources, offers a broad look at the different requirements for immigrants who want to obtain and maintain a green card.

How to Obtain a Green Card
Obtaining lawful permanent resident ("LPR") status, or a "green

card," is another step towards citizenship. In many cases, it is more difficult to obtain LPR status than citizenship.

U.S. immigration laws offer immigrants several ways of applying for a green card, depending on their individual situations. Most require a sponsor who can be a close relative or an employer.

USCIS says applicants must complete at least two forms; an immigrant petition and a Green Card application (Form I-485).

But first they must qualify under at least one of the eight following categories:
- Family
- Employment
- Special Immigrant
- Refugee or Asylee Status
- Human Trafficking and Crime Victims
- Victims of Abuse
- Other Categories such as the Visa Lottery and the Cuban Adjustment Act
- Registry

Green Card for a Family Member
You are a U.S. citizen or lawful permanent resident in the U.S. and you would like to bring a family member to this country. Your understanding of this information Increases the chances of success by making sure you follow USCIS policies and procedures as best you can.

Family Based Visas

The U.S. government allows foreign nationals to obtain legal residence based on their relationship with relatives who are already U.S. citizens or permanent residents.

There are two categories of family relationships: immediate relatives, such as spouses and unmarried children; and other family members described by immigration authorities as "preferences immigrants."

Widows and widowers who were married to American citizens at the time of the citizen's death are also eligible, as long as they can prove that their marriage was not fraudulent.

Green Card for Fiancés and Married Spouses Abroad
A foreign national who is engaged to marry a U.S. Citizen can a obtain K-1 Visa, which allows him or her to travel to the United States on a "non-immigrant status" and marry their petitioner within ninety days after admission.

Both partners must be legally free to marry, and if they have been married before they are required to present proof of their divorce or the death of a previous spouse. If the relationship started and developed on the internet, they must show proof that they met in person at least once in the previous two years.

If the couple were married abroad, the immigrant partner is not eligible for this visa but can be sponsored as an immediate relative through Form I-130, Petition for Alien Relative. Once the petition is approved, the information will be sent to the U.S. Embassy or Consulate in their country of residence.

Medical Examination for a Green Card
Every immigrant applying for lawful permanent resident status

must undergo medical exams and vaccinations for immigration purposes to establish that there are no health issues that would deem the applicant inadmissible to the United States.

The medical tests are required for all eight categories of green card applications and must be performed by designated doctors who then must sign Form I-693 and send it on to USCIS with the results.

Immigrants must schedule their medical tests as close as possible to the filing date of the residence applications in order to make sure the results remain valid, the federal agency notes.

How to Keep a Green Card
Permanent resident status can be lost due to inadvertent mistakes by green card holders, intentional abandonment of their status or deportation orders issued by an immigration judge.

USCIS considers abandonment to move to another country to live there permanently or living abroad for a prolonged period without evidence that the foreign stay is temporary.

Other factors that can negatively affect green card holders is failing to declare income to the U.S. Internal Revenue Service (IRS) or claiming to be "non-immigrants" in their tax returns.

(Source: DANIEL SHOER ROTH. Miami Herald 2019)

CHAPTER 6

DEFINING A LEGALLY VALID MARRIAGE UNDER U.S. IMMIGRATION LAW

"Born in other countries, yet believing you could be happy in this, our laws acknowledge, as they should do, your right to join us in society, conforming, as I doubt not you will do, to our established rules. That these rules shall be as equal as prudential considerations will admit, will certainly be the aim of our legislatures, general and particular."
– Thomas Jefferson

If you are a foreign national married to a U.S. citizen or permanent resident, and plan to apply for a marriage-based visa or green card, you must double check that this marriage meets the following requirements:

- You and your spouse are legally married
- You and your spouse are in a bona fide marriage
- You are married to a U.S. citizen or lawful permanent resident, and
- Neither you nor your spouse are married to anyone else.

We'll explain all of these below.

Requirement of a Legal Marriage

To qualify for a marriage-based visa or green card, you must be legally married. A legal marriage is one that is officially recognized by the government in the country or state where you were married. This usually means that an official record of your marriage has been made or can be obtained from some public office.

Same-sex marriages count for immigration purposes, as of 2013 (the year the Supreme Court issued its decision in U.S. v. Windsor, striking down the federal Defense of Marriage Act (DOMA), which had defined marriage as between a man and a woman). However, not every U.S. state authorizes same-sex marriages. The marriage will need to have taken place in a state or country where such marriages are legally recognized.

Domestic partnerships, in which a couple lives together but have not formalized their relationship, are not normally recognized for immigration purposes. However, if you have lived together in a place that recognizes common law marriages, you may be able to show that you met the requirements for your marriage to be legally recognized in that state or country. If you are in this situation, consult an immigration attorney.

You do not need to have been married in the United States for your marriage to be legal. It is perfectly acceptable if you marry in your home country or elsewhere. A variety of marriage procedures are also recognized, from church weddings to customary tribal practices.

But note that both you and your spouse must have actually attended your wedding ceremony. So-called "proxy" marriages, where another person stands in for the bride or groom, are not recognized by the US government unless the couple later consummates the marriage, meaning they have sexual relations.

If you have not yet married, make sure you are eligible to do so. The state or federal government where you intend to marry may have legal restrictions on who can marry. In the United States, each of the fifty states establishes its own marriage rules. For example, in some states you must be eighteen years of age to marry, while in others you can marry younger if you can have the consent of your parents.

If you and your spouse are related by blood, you'll also need to do some research. You'll find that all states prohibit marrying your sister or brother (sibling), half-sibling, parent, grandparent, great grandparent, child, grandchild, great grandchild, aunt, uncle, niece, or nephew. But some states have additional prohibitions, such as marrying your first cousin.

Finally, you will need to get a document to show you were legally married. The immigration authorities may not accept anything less formal than a marriage certificate issued by a legitimate governmental agency (as opposed to a piece of paper from a church or a ship's captain, for example).

Requirement of a "Bona Fide" Marriage
A bona fide marriage is one in which the two people intend, from the start, to establish a life together as husband and wife. (Or, in the case of same-sex marriages, husband and husband or wife and wife!)

Although marriage can mean different things to different people, one thing is clear: A marriage entered into for the sole purpose of getting the immigrant a green card is not bona fide. It's called a "sham" or "fraudulent" marriage, and uncovering these relationships is a top USCIS priority.

Requirement that You Married a Citizen or Permanent Resident of the United States

There are only two classes of people living in the United States who can obtain permanent residence or green cards for their spouses: U.S. citizens and U.S. lawful permanent residents (green card holders).

Determining Whether Your Spouse is a U.S. Citizen

Your spouse may have become a U.S. citizen in a variety of ways, including:

- Being born in the United States or its territories;
- Becoming a citizen through application and testing (called naturalization); or
- Acquiring or deriving citizenship through a family member. (Acquisition and derivation of citizenship are complex areas of the law. In general, however, people may acquire citizenship by being born abroad to one or two U.S. citizen parents; they may derive citizenship if they become lawful permanent residents first and then their parents are or become U.S. citizens).

Unlike some other countries, the United States does not require that its citizens carry any sort of national identity card. People who are U.S. citizens may have different types of documents that prove their status, such as a birth certificate, a U.S. passport, or a naturalization certificate. Your spouse will need to get a copy of documentary proof of his or her citizenship in order to accompany your application for a US green card.

Determining Whether Your Spouse is a U.S. Lawful Permanent Resident

A lawful permanent resident is someone with a legally obtained green card. This means that the person has a right to live in the United States permanently and may eventually become a U.S. citizen. The spouses of permanent residents are eligible for a green card (although it will take longer than for spouses of U.S. citizens, due to annual limits on the number of available visas).

You should know, however, that the fact that your spouse has a green card now doesn't guarantee that he or she will have it forever. Permanent residence can be lost, for example, if the person makes his or her home outside the United States or commits certain crimes or other acts that cause the immigration authorities to begin removal proceedings and order the person deported. If your spouse lost his or her permanent residence while your application was being decided on, you would also lose your right to immigrate through your marriage.

A green card is not the same thing as a work permit card. If your spouse carries a card with the title Employment Authorization Document, he or she is not a permanent resident.

Requirement That This Is Your and Your Spouse's Only Marriage

Any previous marriages must have ended by legal means – such as death, divorce, or annulment – and you'll have to present the official documents to prove it. Otherwise, the immigration authorities will wonder whether your first marriage is still your active and real one, making your new marriage just a sham to get a green card.

(Source: All Law.com)

CHAPTER 7

MARRIAGE-BASED ADJUSTMENT OF STATUS INTERVIEW

"Let the poor the needy and oppressed of the Earth, and those who want Land, resort to the fertile lands of our western country, the second land of Promise, and there dwell in peace, fulfilling the first and great commandment."
– George Washington

A foreign national spouse of a U.S. citizen who is also inside the United States can generally apply for a green card without leaving the U.S. This process, known as adjustment of status, concludes with an interview. U.S. Citizenship and Immigration Services (USCIS) interviews virtually every applicant for a marriage-based green card. Upon completion of a successful marriage-based adjustment of status interview, the applicant will generally become a permanent resident (green card holder). Every couple should prepare for this interview. Knowing what to expect, what items to take, and how to respond to questions will improve your chances of a quick approval.

After filing a marriage-based Form I-485, Application to Adjust Status, there are generally two appointments. USCIS will schedule a biometrics appointment for the applicant (usually within the first couple of months) and then the interview appointment several months later. USCIS requires both spouses (the applicant and petitioner) to attend the marriage-based adjustment of status interview.

Appointment Notice for Adjustment of Status Interview

You'll know it's time for your interview when USCIS mails the interview appointment notice. Like many other USCIS communications, the appointment notice will be labeled as I-797C Notice of Action.

They mail the notice for your marriage-based adjustment of status interview a few months into the I-485 time-line. You'll have a few weeks to prepare and make travel arrangements (if necessary). Although you mailed your application to a USCIS lockbox location, they will schedule an interview at a local office nearest you. In some areas of the country, this may require a long drive and an overnight stay.

Before the Interview

Review your applications and all supporting documents. Make sure the information is consistent. Has anything changed? Be familiar with the information and ready to answer questions. The USCIS officer will analyze the dates, places of residence, employment and other facts.

Discuss the Facts of Your Relationship

Spend some time with your spouse discussing the history of your relationship. Make sure you remember your initial meeting the same way. Review the facts and circumstances surrounding your relationship, such as where and how you met, how your relationship developed, who proposed, how and how did the family accept your relationship, any special things you like to do together, etc. Don't assume your spouse will have the same answer. It will be embarrassing and even damaging to your case if you provide different answers to the USCIS officer.

Items to Take to Interview

The USCIS appointment notice will include a list of items to take to your adjustment of status interview. Follow the directions on your appointment notice. Until then, the following list will get you prepared for the interview. You should expect to take the following items:

Appointment notice (I-797C, Notice of Action) for your I-485 interview.

Government-Issued Photo ID. Typically your passport (even if expired) but can also be any other government-issued photo ID like a driver's license.

A complete copy of your adjustment of status application packet. In addition to Form I-485, have available any other forms (e.g. I-130, I-130A, I-864, I-131, I-765) you may have submitted.

Originals of any supporting documents that you submitted to USCIS with the adjustment of status application. Especially important examples include birth, marriage and death certificates as well as divorce decrees (if available).

Your passport (unless you are in certain categories such as refugee/asylum).

Any other travel documents, for example your advance parole

permit if you traveled while awaiting your interview.

Doctor's report from your required medical examination on Form I-693 (if you did not submit this report with the original adjustment application).

Copies plus originals of documents showing your shared life, such as a joint lease or mortgage, joint bank account or credit card statements, children's birth certificates, and so on.

Day of Marriage-Based Adjustment of Status Interview

Treat the day like a court appointment or job interview. That starts with the way you dress. Avoid flashy jewelry and body art that might lead a USCIS officer to make negative presumptions about you or your character. Dress professionally.

Be punctual. Although it's likely that you'll have to wait for your interview, arrive at the USCIS office at the time instructed.

The Interview

The USCIS officer will begin the interview by swearing you in. By taking this oath, you've promised to tell the truth, and the consequences are significant for lying to a USCIS officer.

Next, it's likely that the officer will verify your identification documents, such as birth certificates, passports and marriage certificate. Again, take original copies of these important documents. They will be returned to you. The USCIS officer will review some of the basic information on the application with you and your spouse.

The USCIS officer will also likely ask if you have had any life changes that may affect your adjustment of status application.

The officer is looking for anything that may change an answer on your application. Some examples include the birth of a child, new employer, or new address. If your changes include an arrest or troubles with the marriage, speak to an immigration attorney before attending your marriage-based adjustment of status interview.

Interview Questions

The officer will ask you and your spouse about your relationship and married life together. He or she may begin the questioning in a friendly manner, like small talk. Remember, your answers are very relevant to the interview. In a marriage-based adjustment of status interview, the questions may begin to get a little personal. It's the officer's job to confirm that you have a bona fide marriage and that marriage fraud played no role in the application for a green card. Some questions you might expect, but are not limited to:

How, when and where did you meet your spouse?

Where and with whom did your spouse live when you met your spouse?

Who lives at your address now?

What is your spouse's date of birth?

Where did your spouse work when you met him/her?

What type of work does your spouse do?

What is your spouse's work schedule?

How much is spouse's salary?

Are both spouses' salaries deposited into the same bank account?

What bank account do you use?

Did your spouse have a car when you met? What model, color, etc?

Are these the cars you and your spouse currently drive?

If not, when did you and/or your spouse change cars?

If you have cars, how much money is owed on them? How much is the monthly payment?

When did you and your spouse decide to get married? Was there a proposal? Who proposed? When and where did it take place?

Did you and your spouse live together prior to your marriage? Where and how long?

When did you and your spouse move in together?

When did you get married?

If you had a celebration, what food/beverages were served?

Did you and your spouse go on a honeymoon? If yes, where?

Who pays the rent/mortgage? How is it paid? (Do you mail it? Hand-deliver it?)

Where does your landlord live?

How many sleeping rooms does your home have?

Are all the sleeping rooms on the same side of the home?

What size bed do you and your spouse have?

Can you describe the pieces of furniture in your bedroom?

This is a small sampling of possible questions. In practice, USCIS can ask a wide variety of questions to help make a determination if you and your spouse have a bona fide marriage.

Additionally, the USCIS officer will review the I-864 Affidavit of Support and tax documents to ensure the sponsor has sufficient income to meet the requirement.

The typical adjustment of status interview lasts approximately 20-25 minutes. After introductions and swearing in, that doesn't leave much time for questioning. It's also not necessary to memorize answers to any questions. For the most part, the USCIS will ask you questions about your application and ask you to verify or explain certain answers. If you've truthfully answered questions on Form I-485, there's no reason to be anxious.

After the Interview
If everything goes well at your adjustment of status interview, the USCIS officer will approve your I-485 application. In some cases, the officer may be able to place an "I-551" stamp inside your passport. Regardless, USCIS will process the new green card and mail to your address on record.

However, other USCIS officers don't provide a decision at the interview. He or she may tell you that you will receive a decision in the mail. Don't be discouraged. This isn't unusual.

It's also possible that a USCIS officer cannot approve your case because additional evidence is required. If USCIS requests additional evidence, be certain to submit the documentation requested by the deadline issued. USCIS will send you a decision by mail.

If it's been ninety days since your marriage-based adjustment of status interview and you still don't have a decision, schedule an InfoPass appointment with USCIS. It's important to follow up.

Conditional Residence

If the marriage is less than two years old at the time permanent residence is granted, USCIS will issue a two-year conditional green card. The green card holder will need to petition to remove the conditions in the 90-day period that precedes the expiration date on the card. This means that the conditional resident needs to file Form I-751, Petition to Remove Conditions, submitting more proof of a bona fide marriage, and paying another filing fee.

However, if you've reached the two-year anniversary of your marriage since filing the application, make sure the USCIS officer is aware. With at least two years of marriage, USCIS can issue a 10-year permanent green card. This will save you the extra time and expense of removing the conditions later.

(Source: Citizen Path 2018)

CHAPTER 8

CHALLENGING ISSUES FOR IMMIGRANT PARENTS AND THEIR CHILDREN

"Immigrant families have integrated themselves into our communities, establishing deep roots. Whenever they have settled, they have made lasting contributions to the economic vitality and diversity of our communities and our nation. Our economy depends on these hard-working, taxpaying workers. They have assisted America in its economic boom." – Senator Edward M. Kennedy

Immigrant families to Canada as Gary Direnfeld, a social worker would say can face many issues complicating their adjustment to the new host culture. This experience is not isolated to immigrants only in one country abroad, but it's the same here in the United States as well as other European countries.

Often unconsidered is the implications for intra-familial culture clash when children take to the host culture sooner or more wholeheartedly than their parents. Risk of conflict between children and their parents is heightened on issues of socialization with opposite gender friends, developing friends of other cultures, issues of rights and freedoms and expectations for academic performance.

Further, it is important to appreciate that immigrant families come to host country generally seeking to provide a better life for their children than what might have been available in their country of origin. Hence when these parents come up against conflict with their children owing to adaptation, the conflict can be felt by the parent as tremendous disrespect by the child who doesn't understand the parents' rationale and sacrifice in coming to the new country.

While there are common challenges faced between immigrant parents and children of both gender, risk of pregnancy is a potent issue that can intensify concerns for the well-being of girls. In addition, strong cultural imperatives with regard to dress, deportment and socializing with the opposite sex can at times place greater demands on girls than boys.

These differences can erupt into serious fights between daughters and parents. Even when a fight does not erupt, some teenaged girls may seek to lead a double-life; keeping secrets about relationships and even their dress when at school or in the community. Other teenaged girls may seek to subordinate their feelings to the will of their parents only to find themselves depressed and anxious over the difficulty with cultural and family adaptation.

Boys do face cultural imperatives and conflicts too, but the absence of risk of pregnancy can lessen the scrutiny placed upon them by parents. However, the boys may be more subject to high expectations for academic excellence, which may or may not be taken well. If not taken well, boys may come to reject their own family's culture, falling prey to the illusions of freedom from authority by gravitating to counter-culture groups or gangs. This in turn can lead to a risk of conflict with the law and abject academic failure as well as extreme conflict with their family.

The challenge is on the parents to adapt and find reasonable strategies to support cultural expectations in view of the greater likelihood that their children will be affected and changed by the new host culture. It is less a question of whether the children will be changed by the host culture, but rather how and to what degree.

Further, some immigrant parents may hail from cultures where the norm is to tell a child what to do and expect obedience. This quickly erodes for the children socialized particularly in western culture where individual freedom is valued and rewarded. Thus those parents who adjust and develop strategies that minimize the risk of conflict with their children stand the opportunity to remain more influential in their children's lives than those parents who rely solely upon control strategies.

While not nagging their children, sharing stories as to why parents chose to immigrate and their hopes for their family's future can inform their children as to their family aspirations. Further, when parents invite their children to engage in a dialogue about the differences between their respective lives non-judgmentally, parents and children may be apprised of their respective experiences and may be in a better position to discuss differences between themselves.

The challenge here is for the parents to develop skills that rely more upon influence than control. This can also be facilitated by participation and enjoyment of cultural activities and inviting their children's new friends to join in. Co-opting children's friends can serve as a better way of maintaining family integrity than isolating from friends.

(Source: SWHELPER 2017: Author Gary Direnfeld, MSW)

CHAPTER 9

THE IMMIGRANT ENTREPRENEUR'S SURVIVAL GUIDE: 5 HACKS FOR NAVIGATING U.S. IMMIGRATION INSANITY

"Citizenship to me is more than a piece of paper. Citizenship is also about character. I am an American. We're just waiting for our country to recognize it." – Jose Antonio Vargas

1. If You're Here, Stay Here

Especially if you're from a high-risk country, plan your life and your business so that once you get here, you can stay in the United States as long as possible. There are lots of legal strategies for lengthening your course of study, changing your visa status, or extending your stay. Take advantage of all of them.

Why do this? Because every interaction with U.S. immigration – especially at the border – is a point of visibility, and a potential attack vector. Every interface increases the risk of a bad consequence. Reducing visibility and minimizing the attack surface are high priorities right now. Stay in low-friction mode.

If you're outside the United States, get here if you can. If you can't, stay where you are, and play the long game. Do everything possible to continue building your business from there. Lots of startup activities, like R&D, prototyping, and investor contact, can be done remotely. For now, minimize your interface with U.S. immigration – a high-risk activity that can harm your long-term prospects. Treat it like other business risks, and bide your time.

2. Make a Plan B, and Be Ready to Pivot

Think through what could happen if some demented new change in U.S. immigration policy forces you to leave the United States, makes it impossible to enter, or both. How will it impact your business? Do you have a place to go, a work-from-any-where strategy, and a mobilization plan for your team?

Hopefully you won't ever need your emergency plan, but it's really important to have one. It's reassuring to your market, your investors, and your people. Most importantly, it gives YOU peace of mind that you can handle the unexpected. These immigration surprises come up like tornadoes – they knock everyone off guard and leave them scrambling. A little forethought can keep you calm and focused on what matters.

3. Get Expert Guidance

U.S. immigration law is already complicated and unpredictable, even without these new, insane, unlawful enforcement actions popping up everywhere. Your U.S. immigration attorney is your best friend right now. Choose an experienced attorney who specializes in startups, and invest in a professional consult about your specific situation.

Ask the attorney to help you plan your visa status strategically for the future. Get advice on all the visas you might qualify for, and how to sequence them, if one doesn't work out. Ask about your worst-case scenarios, their consequences, and their remedies. Get scripts for international travel to optimize your U.S. entry process.

Chance definitely favors the prepared mind here, and a good attorney is the best preparation tool you've got.

4. Scrub the Data on Your Devices Before Entering the United States

OK, sometimes you have to travel. Your papers are in order, you know what to say to the immigration inspector, and you've done everything you can to ease your U.S. entry process.

So what do you do when the inspector seizes your devices, demands your passwords, and threatens to deny you entry if you refuse?

Legally, you're not required to disclose your passwords. This is NOT a lawful ground for denial of entry.

But when you're standing there in customs, jet-lagged and scared, it's really hard to say no. You don't feel like playing chicken with authority figures. And if you do get denied entry, even though it's unlawful, there's not a lot of recourse.

So what happens if you say yes? Well . . . very bad things. U.S. Immigration uses a "data vacuum cleaner" to suck every byte of data off your device within seconds. They can then paw through all your email, social media, apps, photos, and documents at their leisure. Apple, Google, Facebook, and most apps have world-class encryption, but it won't do you a bit of good if you've voluntarily surrendered your most private and personal information. And once the government has it, they have it forever.

This is a really scary scenario! Many attorneys and privacy experts now recommend leaving your devices at home when you travel. However, that's not a realistic option for most people.

One workable alternative, is to put ALL your information in the cloud, then scrub your device clean. Delete all the browsers and apps. Optimally, you can reset it to factory settings. At that point you can hand it over, and even disclose your password, without compromising your personal information.

5. Play the Long Game

U.S. immigration insanity is just one piece of a much larger puzzle you're solving as an entrepreneur. It creates huge uncertainty and inconvenience in the short term, but it's a business risk that can be quantified and planned for to a certain extent.

Continue working toward your long-term business vision. Act with confidence that our immigration craziness is temporary and short-lived, but plan for the possibility that it's not.

Make a long-range U.S. immigration plan and go about executing it.

Finally, stay alert, stay agile, and be ready to adapt. As an entrepreneur, these skills are second nature to you. They're going to come in handy as you navigate the "new normal." Please, keep fighting the good fight! We need you here now, more than you know.

(Source: Mary M. Kearney. Licensed Immigration attorney 2017)

CHAPTER 10

VISA BASICS FOR FOREIGN ENTREPRENEURS COMING TO THE U.S.

"I've always argued that this country has benefited immensely from the fact that we draw people from all over the world." – Alan Greenspan

Non-immigrant foreign entrepreneurs who want to start businesses in the U.S. often – and rightly – have visa-related concerns. A typical question: "What kind of visa do I need to start my business?

This resource provides a brief answer to that question.

Visa Waiver

Allows an individual to come to the U.S. for 90 days. No extension or change of status is allowed. Allows attendance at business meetings and other passive business development activities. Does not allow compensation from U.S. sources.

B-1

Business visitor: Allows admission for up to six months. Can be extended, and permits a change to a different immigration status. Allows passive business activities, but not productive work in the U.S. or receipt of any U.S.-based remuneration.

However, expenses can be reimbursed. Must benefit a foreign, rather than U.S. business.

E-2

Investor: Requires that a U.S. entity be set up and that a substantial investment made into that entity. Takes several months to obtain and is comparatively expensive. Applies to investors from countries with which the U.S. has applicable treaties. Applies for two years. May be extended for additional two-year periods without limitation.

H-1B

Specialty occupation: Allows a U.S. employer to hire an individual for a specified complex or unique job for a period of up to three years because the position cannot be filled easily from the workforce available in the U.S. Typically can be extended to six years. The individual can form a business in the U.S. but cannot work for it. Note that USCIS gives H-1B cases particularly careful scrutiny.

L-1

Intracompany Transferee: Requires setting up a U.S. company that is a subsidiary or affiliate of an existing foreign company. The individual must have been working for the foreign company for at least one year prior to the transfer. The individual must be working in the U.S. in a managerial, executive or special-ized-knowledge capacity. Valid for five years (special-knowledge employees) or seven years (managers or executives). "Dual intent" visa, meaning the holder can apply for a green card without jeopardizing the visa.

(Source: Dana H. Shultz, Attorney at Law. 2009)

Visa Basics for Foreign Entrepreneurs, Part 2:
What Constitutes Work?

In Visa Basics for Foreign Entrepreneurs Coming to the U.S., I discussed certain immigration statuses (visa waiver, B-1 and H-1B visas) that permit a non-resident alien to take a passive role in a business (such as forming it) but not to work for it. This article discusses the boundary between permissible passive activities and prohibited work.

Let's assume that the new business is formed as a corporation. Being a shareholder certainly is a passive activity. Being a director (board member) typically should be a passive activity, too, because directors' role is one of oversight and approval (elect officers, approve major transactions, etc.), rather than running the business.

Being an officer is not permitted, however. Officers are directly responsible for running the business, thus they inherently are actively involved in working for it.

Summary if you are a non-resident alien who must keep his or her activities for a business passive: It's OK to be a shareholder and a director, but don't become an officer, employee or independent contractor of the business or do any additional work for it.

(Source: Dana H. Shultz, Attorney at Law. 2011)

Remember, the U.S. Department of State offers more-detailed information starting at its Temporary Workers Visas page.

PART THREE

LEARNING IS FOR LIVING

CHAPTER 11

WHAT IMMIGRATION ATTORNEYS WANT YOU TO KNOW

"We came to America, either ourselves or in the persons of our ancestors, to better the ideals of men, to make them see finer things than they had seen before, to get rid of the things that divide and to make sure of the things that unite." – Woodrow Wilson

If you or a loved one is facing deportation back to your home country, it could be for any number of reasons. Since the 9/11 attacks, we have seen an increase in the number of people deported from the United States, and most immigration attorneys are willing to help you fight this process so that you can stay in the country. If a challenge needs to be made to the underlying factual basis of the deportation proceedings, for instance a criminal charge, attorneys may be able to go back to the criminal court and try to obtain a more favorable disposition. If your case needs to be appealed, our referral team of attorneys have the experience as litigator and appellate advocate and will serve you well.

Don't Try to Navigate the Complicated World of United States Immigration Alone

As an immigrant, trying to navigate the complicated world of United States immigration and citizenship alone can be tough. The immigration attorneys we work with and those who specialize in this area can handle your case and help you in many areas including with residence permits, asylum issues, employment – or family-based immigration, and deportation defense. Don't lose your right to live and work in this great country.

Reach out to us to see how we can help you. contact@beinformedimmigrant.com

Asylum

If you face persecution back in your home country, you may be eligible for asylum in the United States. Don't go it alone. Find out how you can greatly increase your chances of success while trying to stay in the United States through a well-crafted asylum application done on your behalf by one of our referring immigration attorneys.

Companies Hiring Immigrants

As your company grows, you may want to hire foreign workers to help your company take advantage of the diversity of skills immigrants offer. Under current immigration law, you can apply for a non-immigrant visa so as to allow that individual to come to, or remain in, the United States. Later, you can sponsor that person for permanent resident status. We have immigration attorneys who specialize in this area and are available to help you institute an intelligent visa strategy that can help you maximize your chances of success with USCIS.

Immigration Delay Litigation

A number of immigrants who have called us for referral purposes tell us that Info Pass appointments, calling the USCIS 1-800 number and sending letter after letter does not do good most of the time when trying to get USCIS to act on an application.

Have you been waiting too long for naturalization or for your green card? Learn how asserting your rights in federal court through an immigration attorney can lead to the one thing you want – action – from USCIS. We have immigration attorneys who will work on your behalf until you case is successfully adjudicated.

Reach out to us to see how we can help you. contact@beinformedimmigrant.com

I-9 Compliance

Immigrants who want to work in the United States must have authorization to do so. Federal statutes and regulations, as well as an increasing number of state laws, govern this complex area of the law. The verification process can be complicated and confusing. The immigration lawyers we work with liaise with both employers and foreign-born workers to ensure compliance with applicable laws.

CHAPTER 12

A BASIC REQUIREMENT TO GET A GREEN CARD HAS CHANGED – AND IT HELPS LEGAL IMMIGRANTS

"Whatever America hopes to bring to pass in the world must first come to pass in the heart of America." – Dwight D. Eisenhower

The U.S. Citizenship and Immigration Services updated a key requirement to obtain a green card effective Nov. 1, 2018.

The policy changes announced this week will affect the medical and vaccination examination for immigration purposes, which makes sure there are no health issues that would deem the applicant inadmissible to the United States.

The medical examination is an indispensable requirement for all foreigners filing for adjustment of status to that of a lawful permanent resident. The results are submitted to USCIS through Form I-693.

According to the latest USCIS Policy Manual Update, Form I-693 must be signed by a USCIS designated civil surgeon no later than sixty days before filing the underlying application for an immigration benefit.

Additionally, the form will remain valid for a two-year-period that will begin to count from the date it was signed by the doctor.

Previously, the doctor was not required to sign the exam's results so close to the filing date of the application. This created a problem for many applicants because by the time their immigration benefit was adjudicated, the I-693 was no longer valid. To overcome this hurdle, the lawful person was required to obtain an updated medical report.

The goal of the new rule is to "enhance operational efficiencies and reduce the number of requests to applicants for an updated Form I-693," said the migration agency.

The revised policy maximizes "the period of time Form I-693 will be valid while the underlying application is under USCIS review," the agency said, specifying that its officers will have leeway to request a new I-693 within the two-year period if they have "reason to believe an applicant may be inadmissible on the health-related grounds."

"Delays in adjudicating the underlying application will also be reduced if fewer requests for updated Forms I-693 are necessary," said the immigration agency, which lately has been revising guidelines to strengthen the enforcement priorities of the Department of Homeland Security.

With stricter deadlines, it is important that green card applicants calculate well sufficient time for the performance of laboratory testing or additional testing required before submitting the results of the medical examination, which must be completed, signed and sealed by the designated physician.

(Source: DANIEL SHOER ROTH. Miami Herald 2018)

CHAPTER 13

BIGGEST MISTAKES IN THE K-1 VISA PROCESS

"Remember, remember always, that all of us, you and I especially, are descended from immigrants and revolutionists." – Franklin D. Roosevelt

The K-1 fiancé visa is one of the most requested U.S. visas. The U.S. Department of State issues the K-1 to the foreign national fiancés of U.S. citizens for the purpose of entering the United States for marriage. Once married, the foreign national may adjust status to permanent resident (green card holder). However, mistakes in the K-1 visa process can ruin those plans. Minor oversights may only delay the process, but other mistakes can create long-term immigration problems.

Although most visa requests are granted, it's good to know the common pitfalls that caused problems for others. We've outlined five of the biggest mistakes in the K-1 visa process. Before preparing Form I-129F, Petition for Alien Fiancé, review these avoidable problems.

Submitting a Poorly Prepared Petition
Sometimes it's the small things that can significantly delay a petition or even cause a denial. In most cases, simple errors and omissions in the Form I-129F will cause a rejection. Although

the petitioner can easily resubmit the petition, it generally creates a significant delay in the K-1 visa process. Each year USCIS rejects thousands of forms because people simply forget to sign them.

Take the time to provide accurate and truthful answers on the petition. Read the I-129F instructions thoroughly so that you understand the intent of the question and how your answers may affect the outcome.

Not Disclosing IMBRA Facts

The International Marriage Broker Regulation Act (IMBRA) of 2005 is a U.S. law intended to provide protections for immigrants and U.S. citizens. Relationships arranged through IMBs can potentially create volatile situations. Foreign nationals – often women – seek entry to the United States. U.S. citizens – often men – seek a marriage. Unfortunately, the leverage that the U.S. citizen holds over the intending immigrant can be the impetus for some abusive situations. The basic provisions of the IMBRA include:

- Prohibits the marketing of any client under the age of 18.
- Requires IMB to perform a background check of the U.S. client and share the findings with the information with the foreign national in the foreign client's primary language.
- Requires that a U.S. citizen disclose certain crimes when filing Form I-129F, Petition for Alien Fiancé.
- Puts limits on the number of times a U.S. citizen can petition a foreign fiancé.

The law itself could force immigration officials to deny a K-1 visa. If the U.S. citizen has failed to share information about a criminal history or past petitions with the foreign national fiancé, the disclosure of the information to the foreign national could result in a canceled engagement.

Immigration officials will collect the U.S. citizen's fingerprints as part of the K-1 visa process.

Evidence of Eligibility for K-1

In addition to "being" eligible, the couple must present evidence of eligibility. Failing to present decent evidence of eligibility is one of the more common mistakes in the K-1 visa process. For the foreign national to qualify for the fiancé visa, the couple must meet the following conditions. They must:

- Have met in-person at least once within the last two years; and
- Intend to marry within ninety days of the foreign national entering; and
- Be legally able to marry in the state where the wedding will be held;
- Have a good faith relationship that's led to marriage proposal; and
- Include a U.S. citizen fiancé petitioner (not a lawful permanent resident) that is petitioning the foreign national.

Not Being Prepared for K-1 Interview

In addition to the evidence in the I-129F visa petition, immigration officials want proof that your engagement is the real thing. Marriage is one of the most abused paths to permanent residence. Therefore, USCIS and consular officers will look for factors that can be red flags for marriage fraud.

Factors that can trigger additional questioning include:
- Engaged a very short time after initial meeting.
- Significant cultural differences.
- Large difference in age.
- Different religions.
- No common spoken language.
- Very little physical time together.

Most people have nothing to worry about. However, it's extremely helpful to understand the types of questions that immigration officials will ask the K-1 applicant. Some applicants who are surprised by the questions may appear guarded or anxious. Most K-1 applicants will interview without the U.S. spouse. Take the time to review typical questions and be prepared for the interview. Read K-1 Fiancé Visa Interview Questions.

Passing the 90-Day Deadline
Once the foreign national's K-1 visa is approved and he or she enters the United States, there's a 90-day deadline to marry and adjust status to permanent resident. This is an extremely tight deadline to plan a wedding and submit some complicated paperwork.

The K-1 visa process stipulates that the foreign national must marry the U.S. citizen within ninety days of entering the U.S. For most, this time-line makes it difficult to have a large wedding at a popular venue. Coordinating travel for immediate family members will be challenging enough. Therefore, it may be more practical to plan a simple ceremony. If you would like to celebrate with a larger group of family and friends, plan a reception or party at a later date.

What's more, the K-1 visa holder must file Form I-485, Application to Adjust Status, soon after the wedding if he/she will stay in the United States. The adjustment of status package will include other forms as well. The typical adjustment of status package based on a K-1 entry includes the following forms:

- I-485, Application to Register Permanent Residence or Adjust Status
- I-864, Affidavit of Support
- I-693, Report of Medical Examination and Vaccination Record
- I-765, Application for Employment Authorization
- I-131, Application for Travel Document

For more detailed information about applying for the green card, read Adjustment of Status Through a K-1 Visa Entry.

Other Mistakes in the K-1 Visa Process

Of course, it should go without saying that the misrepresentation of facts will result in a visa denial. Being truthful throughout the K-1 visa process is important. Even if immigration officials don't initially catch a lie, it can haunt the applicant later. For example, at the time of applying for a green card, USCIS officers may review previous visa cases. They will deny the green card if new information makes it apparent that a visa was fraudulently obtained previously. If at any point you feel as though a truthful answer on a visa application might be problematic, contact an immigration lawyer for guidance.

(Source: Citizen Path 2018)

CHAPTER 14

IMMIGRANTS SEEKING PERMANENT GREEN CARDS THROUGH MARRIAGE MAY HAVE ONE LESS HURDLE

"Let us raise a standard to which the wise and honest can repair." – George Washington

The U.S. Citizenship and Immigration Services (USCIS) has revised one of its procedures for immigrants who got their green cards through marriage with U.S. citizens.

Green cards issued for those immigrants are normally conditional and are only valid for two years.

After that, those seeking permanent residence must prove their marriage was not intended to break the immigration laws and therefore is not fraudulent.

This process, known as a petition to Remove Conditions on Permanent Residence Based on Marriage, requires Form I-751 and most likely an interview with a USCIS official to demonstrate eligibility to remove such conditions.

The interviews often make couples nervous because they are questioned, frequently separately, about intimate details of their lives in order to test the legitimacy of their marriages.

But a new policy memorandum issued by USCIS provides some guidelines that agency officials can use to decide whether to waive that interview requirement.

USCIS announced this week that adjudicators are now able to waive this important requirement if they are satisfied that:

- There is sufficient evidence about the authenticity of the marriage that proves it clearly was not entered into in order to evade immigration laws;
- There is no indication of fraud or misrepresentation in the Form I-751 or the supporting documentation;
- USCIS has already interviewed the main petitioner of Form I-751 (this is relevant for cases received after Dec. 10, 2018);
- There are no complex facts or issues that require an interview to clarify.

"When determining whether to waive an interview, the considerations listed above apply regardless of whether the Form I-751 is filed as a joint petition or as a waiver of the joint filing requirement," the new guideline notes. "Cases involving fraud or national security concerns must be referred to the Fraud Detection and National Security Directorate according to local procedures."

(Source: DANIEL SHOER ROTH. Miami Herald 2019)

CHAPTER 15

DEMOCRATS INTRODUCE A BILL THAT OFFER MILLIONS OF IMMIGRANTS

A PATHWAY TO PERMANENT RESIDENCY

"The United States should be an asylum for the persecuted lovers of civil and religious liberty." – Thomas Paine

House Bill H.R. 6 seeks to provide under the Deferred Action for Childhood Arrivals (DACA), Temporary Protected Status (TPS), and Deferred Enforced Departure (DED) permanent residency and a pathway to citizenship.

H.R. 6, also titled Dream and Promise Act, is sponsored by three members of Congress; Rep. Lucille Roybal-Allard (CA), Rep. Nydia Velazquez (NY), and Rep. Yvette Clarke (NY).

House Speaker Nancy Pelosi has endorsed the bill, tweeting: "It's time to Protect The Dream for America's brave dreamers & recipients of TPS & DED by passing #HR6, the Dream & Promise Act."

DACA protects immigrants (DREAMers) brought illegally into the US from deportation, while TPS gives temporary protection from deportation to nationals of countries that the Department of Homeland Security has determined to be unsafe after natural disasters or armed conflict. It currently includes nationalities of the following ten countries; El Salvador, Haiti, Honduras, Nepal, Nicaragua, Somalia, Sudan, South Sudan, Syria, and Yemen. DED on the other hand currently only offers protection to Liberian citizens.

The Dream and Promise Act, if passed into law, would give TPS and DED immigrants an immediate pathway to a green card, by first giving recipients conditional permanent resident status for ten years. Those who got a degree from a recognized university (or completed two years in good standing of a bachelor's or technical program), served for two years in the military, or worked for three years would be eligible to apply for permanent residency immediately.

It is estimated that H.R. 6 would grant about 2.5 million immigrants with a pathway to permanent residency and eventually to citizenship if passed into law. While the bill could pass in the Democrats-controlled House of Representatives, it is unlikely that the Senate – currently controlled by Republicans – would take up the bill in its current form. President Donald Trump, who has threatened to end the DACA and TPS programs as well as limit immigration to the US in general, would also almost certainly not sign the bill.

(Source: Irungu Thairu. *Mwakilishi*, 2019)

CHAPTER 16

LEGAL IMMIGRANTS WHO ABUSE PUBLIC BENEFITS ARE NOW MORE LIKELY TO BE DEPORTED

"It says something about our country that people around the world are willing to leave their homes and leave their families and risk everything to come to America. Their talent and hard work and love of freedom have helped make America the leader of the world. And our generation will ensure that America remains a beacon of liberty and the most hope fill society this world has ever known." – George W. Bush

New Trump administration guidelines that expand the list of reasons for which immigrants can be summoned before an immigration judge to start deportation procedures took effect Monday, Oct. 1, 2018.

The updated list, had been announced in July 2018 by the U.S. Citizenship and Immigration Service (USCIS), which includes the option of deporting legal immigrants if they violate federal or state programs related to "the reception of public benefits."

The rules give immigration officials more leeway to issue Notices to Appear, or NTAs – a document issued to non-citizens instructing them to appear in immigration court. The NTAs traditionally mark the beginning of a deportation process.

Starting October 1 2018, USCIS agents are be able to issue an NTA for a wider range of cases involving evidence of fraud, criminal activity or when a foreign citizen is denied an immigration benefit and therefore loses legal status to remain in the United States.

The USCIS policy memorandum states its purpose is to align with Trump's executive order "for enhancing public safety," which "articulated the priorities for the removal of aliens from the United States."

"For too long, USCIS officers uncovering instances of fraudulent or criminal activity had been limited in their ability to help ensure U.S. immigration laws are faithfully executed," agency Director L. Francis Cissna said.

The new procedures, he added, give immigration officers more freedom and offers them "clear guidance they need and deserve to support the enforcement priorities established by the president, keep our communities safe, and protect the integrity of our immigration system from those seeking to exploit it.

Another news release issued announced the implementation of the new policy on NTAs noted that USCIS will send "denial letters for status-impacting applications that ensures benefit seekers are provided adequate notice when an application for a benefit is denied."

The immigration agency said the revised guidelines are designed to strengthen the enforcement priorities of the Department of Homeland Security, which made public a proposal to keep immigrants from obtaining permanent residence or green cards if they receive certain public benefits.

Under the new guidelines, USCIS adjudicators are required to issue NTAs in the following categories:

- Cases in which fraud or false representation is substantiated.
- Cases in which immigrants have abused some of the public benefits available to them.
- Cases in which immigrants have been accused or convicted of a criminal offense, even if criminal conduct was not the basis for the denial.
- USCIS will be allowed to refer cases involving serious criminal activity to ICE before adjudication of an immigration benefit request pending before USCIS without issuing an NTA.
- Cases in which USCIS denies an Application for Naturalization on good moral character grounds because of a criminal offense.
- Cases in which, upon the denial of an application or petition, an applicant is unlawfully present in the United States.

The USCIS announcement added that it will continue to "prioritize cases of individuals with criminal records, fraud, or national security concerns."

(Source: DANIEL SHOER ROTH. Miami Herald 2018)

PART FOUR

DO WHAT YOU CAN WHILE YOU CAN

CHAPTER 17

KNOW YOUR RIGHTS
A GUIDE TO YOUR RIGHTS WHEN INTERACTING WITH LAW ENFORCEMENT

"More than any other nation on earth, America has constantly drawn strength and spirit from wave after wave of immigrants. In each generation, they have proved to be the most restless, the most adventurous, the most innovative, the most industrious of people. Bearing different memories, honoring different heritages, they have strengthened our economy, enriched our culture, renewed our promise of freedom and opportunity for all . . ."
– Bill Clinton

YOU HAVE RIGHTS regardless of your immigration status. You may be at risk of being deported if you are undocumented, if you are a non-citizen with a criminal history, if you are on parole or have a prior deportation order. To protect yourself, your family and your community you must KNOW YOUR RIGHTS.

Knowledge is power. Act NOW. Do not wait. Be prepared.
Most of the information on the guide below comes from Catholic church immigrant and refugee ministry platform. Know your rights information is part of Catholic church efforts

to support Pope Francis' "Share the Journey" initiative, a global Catholic campaign to aid migrants and refugees that was launched Sept. 27, 2017. For more resources, visit clini-clegal.org.

The information is focused in helping immigrants cope with fear and uncertainty

This guide contains:
- What you need to know and what to do when encountering immigration agents, the police or FBI in different places.
- Information about how to read a warrant.
- Twelve things for you and your family to remember in ANY situation.
- Your Emergency Planning Checklist.
- Your Emergency Contact Information Sheet.
- Your plan for what to do if a loved one calls you from an immigration detention center or police station.
- Your Workplace Planning Checklist.

WHERE: YOUR HOME
WHAT YOU NEED TO KNOW: To enter your home, immigration officers or the police need either 1) a valid warrant signed by a judge or magistrate, or 2) your permission.
- DO NOT OPEN THE DOOR. Opening the door could mean you give the officers permission to enter your home.
- A warrant DOES NOT mean you have to answer questions.
- If immigration officers or the police are questioning you and you wish to remain silent, say out loud that you wish to remain silent or show the officials your Know Your Rights card if you have one available. Find one in our website: www.

beinformedimmigrant.com or use the one that is provided in this book.

WHAT TO DO:

STEP 1
DO NOT OPEN THE DOOR.

STEP 2
ASK FOR IDENTIFICATION.
Officers may try to trick or intimidate you to get into your house. Look through a window to see their ID. Do not be caught off guard and open the door.

STEP 3
Ask the officials if they have a warrant.

STEP 4
If the officers do not have a warrant, they do not have the right to enter your home. You can ask them to leave. You have a right to see a warrant. Ask the officials to slide it under the door or put it up to a window. Read the warrant. If it does not have the required information, it is not valid. The officers cannot enter your home.

STEP 5
If officers enter your home (with or without a valid warrant) inform them if there are children, elderly or sick people in the house. If they enter without a valid warrant, say that you do not consent. Pay close attention. After they have left, write

down what happened in detail. Include the type of officers, their names, badge numbers and the contact information of any witnesses.

READING A WARRANT

How to Read a Warrant

- Officers may only enter your home or workplace with 1) a VALID warrant, or 2) your permission or the permission of your employer. (Valid means that a warrant has authority and must be obeyed.)
- For a warrant to be valid, it must contain certain information.
- Below, please find samples of the different types of warrants and information they must contain to be valid.
- Warrants may look different depending on your state or location. This means that information required to make a warrant valid may appear in different orders or look different from the samples below.

If officers do not have permission to enter and they do not have a warrant or a valid warrant, it is your right to ask them to leave!

SEARCH WARRANT

A valid search warrant:

- Must be signed by a judge, justice of the peace or magistrate.
- Must state the address to be searched.
- Must state in detail the area to be searched. In some cases, search warrants may be many pages long describing locations to be searched.
- Look for other information that might make the warrant

invalid, such as being out of date.

- If the officer does not have a valid warrant you can say, "This is not a valid warrant. You may not enter. Please leave."
- If the officer has a valid warrant, you must allow them to enter your home. When they enter say, "I do not consent to this search." This should limit where they are allowed to search.
- Observe where the officers search. Observe if they search in areas that the warrant does not list. Repeat that you do not consent to the search. If an officer takes any of your property, ask for a receipt.

ARREST WARRANT

A valid arrest warrant:

- Must be signed by a judge, justice of the peace or magistrate.
- Must state the name of the person to be arrested.
- Must describe the person to be arrested.
- Look for other information that might make the warrant invalid, such as being out of date.
- If the officer does not have a valid warrant, you can say, "This is not a valid warrant. You may not enter. Please leave."
- If the officer has a valid arrest warrant and the person named in the warrant is there, that person should go outside to meet the officer. Close the door behind them. If the person named in the warrant is not there, tell the officer that the person is not there. And do not open the door.

WARRANT OF REMOVAL/DEPORTATION

(Immigration Warrant)

- A warrant of removal or deportation (an immigration warrant) DOES NOT give an officer the right to enter your home. Say, "You do not have the right to enter with this warrant. Please leave."

WHERE: THE STREET OR A PUBLIC AREA

WHAT YOU NEED TO KNOW:

- Do not run if you see immigration officers or the police approaching you.
- If you are stopped on the street or in a public area, you have the right to remain silent and not answer questions.
- In some states, the law says that you must tell the police your name if they ask. See the emergency plan elsewhere in this chapter for more information and to make a plan that is best for you.
- In general, an officer needs a warrant to arrest you. In some situations you could be arrested if the officer has evidence you do not have legal status or if you have committed a crime.

WHAT TO DO:

- In some situations, officers have the right to search you to make sure you are not carrying weapons or illegal materials. Do not resist or fight back.
- If you are in an airport or near the United States border, you may be questioned or detained without a warrant. You still have the right to remain silent.
- In the past, immigration officers would not stop or detain

people in certain public places, including schools, hospitals, places of worship, funerals, weddings, public religious ceremonies or public demonstrations (a march, rally or procession). This may change in the future. Also remember that you could be stopped on your way to or from these places.

STEP 1

Before you say anything, INCLUDING YOUR NAME, ask, "Am I free to go?"

STEP 2

If the officer says yes, walk away slowly. If the officer says no, do not walk away.

STEP 3

You have the right to remain silent. Do not provide any information about your immigration status, where you were born, or how/when you came to the United States. Do not show any documents from your home country. Say out loud if you wish to remain silent or show the officer your Know Your Rights card if you have one available. Find one in our website: www.beinformedimmigrant.com or use the one provided in this book.

STEP 4

If the officer searches you, arrests or detains you, remain calm. Do not resist or fight. If you are searched, say, "I do not consent to this search."

WHERE: YOUR WORKPLACE

WHAT YOU NEED TO KNOW:

- To enter your workplace, immigration officers or the police need either 1) a valid warrant, or 2) the permission of your employer.
- Do not run. If you run, it may lead to you being arrested or detained.
- A warrant DOES NOT mean you have to answer questions.
- If immigration officers or the police are questioning you and you wish to remain silent, say out loud that you wish to remain silent or show the officers your Know Your Rights card if you have one available.
- Make sure to complete the workplace checklist provided elsewhere in this chapter.

WHAT TO DO:

STEP 1

Make sure to have a plan in place with workers in the event of a raid.

STEP 2

If your employer is not present or if your employer has given permission to the officers to enter, have the person you have chosen to speak with officers in a raid ASK FOR IDENTIFICATION.

STEP 3

The person should read the warranty carefully and your co-workers determine if it is valid. Remember, the officers may try to trick, intimidate or frighten you.

STEP 4

If officers enter your workplace, you have the right to remain silent. Do not provide any information about your immigration status, where you were born, or how/ when you came to the United States. Do not show any documents from your home country. Say out loud if you wish to remain silent or show the officer your Know Your Rights card if you have one available with you.

STEP 5

If the officer searches you, arrests or detains you, remain calm and do not fight back. If you are searched, say, "I do not consent to this search."

WHERE: YOUR CAR
WHAT YOU NEED TO KNOW:

- Different laws apply when you are stopped in your car than if you are stopped on the street.
- If you are stopped at a border checkpoint, officers may search your car.

WHAT TO DO:
STEP 1

Pull the car over and turn it off. Put on the overhead lights in the car. Put your hands on the steering wheel where the officer can see them.

STEP 2

When asked, follow the officer's instructions and provide your license, registration and proof of insurance. If you do not have a license or registration, do not provide false documents or lie.

STEP 3

If the officer asks to search your car you can say "No, I do not consent to a search." In some situations, the officer can search your car without your consent and without a warrant. You should still say that you do not consent to a search.

STEP 4

You have the right to remain silent. Do not provide any information about your immigration status, where you were born, or how/when you came to the United States. Do not show any documents from your home country. Say out loud if you wish to remain silent or show the officer your Know Your Rights card if you have one available on you.

WHERE: IN POLICE CUSTODY/JAIL
WHAT YOU NEED TO KNOW:

- Arrests, charges and convictions can affect your immigration status.
- If you are at risk for deportation, you should avoid contact with the police.
- You have the right to make a phone call.
- You have the right to remain silent. Being arrested or detained by the police does not mean you have to answer questions.
- You have the right to speak to an attorney. You should request an attorney and one will be provided for you.
- You have the right to refuse to sign anything before speaking with your attorney.

WHAT TO DO:

- You should not discuss your immigration information with

ANYONE other than your attorney while you are with the police. This includes where you were born, how/when you came to the United States or any criminal history. Say out loud if you wish to remain silent or show your Know Your Rights card if you have one available on you.

- In some cases, the police may contact immigration or hand you over to immigration. This is why you must not to discuss your immigration information with ANYONE besides your attorney.
- You must tell your attorney about your immigration status and your criminal history.

STEP 1

Request a phone call so that you can call your emergency contact (family member, attorney, religious or community organization, consulate). See details elsewhere in this chapter - how to create an emergency plan.

STEP 2

Do not discuss your immigration status with ANYONE other than your attorney. This includes where you were born, how you came to the U.S., or your criminal background. Say out loud if you wish to remain silent or show your Know Your Rights card. Anything you say can be used against you.

STEP 3

Do not sign anything without speaking to your attorney. If you are being asked to sign something, say, "I will not sign anything until I speak with my attorney." Ask questions if you do not understand what you are being asked to sign.

STEP 4

Make sure to request your own copy of all documents your attorney submits to the judge as part of your case.

WHERE: IN AN IMMIGRATION DETENTION CENTER
WHAT YOU NEED TO KNOW:

- You have the right to make a phone call.
- You have the right to call your consulate.
- You have the right to remain silent. Being detained does not mean you have to answer questions.
- You have the right to speak to an attorney or accredited representative. You or a family member must contact the attorney or accredited representative. This will not be provided for you automatically.
- You have the right to refuse to sign anything before speaking with your attorney or accredited representative.
- When you speak to an attorney or accredited representative, it is essential that you tell them about any prior arrests or criminal history even if someone told you it was erased from your record.
- A person at risk of deportation should never visit a detention center or voluntarily interact with immigration officers.

WHAT TO DO:
STEP 1

Request a phone call so that you can call your emergency contact (family member, attorney, religious or community organization, consulate). See details elsewhere in this chapter - how to create an emergency plan.

STEP 2

Call your consulate for assistance.

STEP 3

Do not provide information to ANYONE other than your attorney or accredited representative about your immigration status, where you were born, how/when you came to the United States or your criminal background. Say out loud if you wish to remain silent or show your Know Your Rights card. Anything you say can be used against you.

STEP 4

You have the right to refuse to sign anything before speaking with your attorney. If you are being asked to sign something, say, "I will not sign anything until I speak with my attorney/ accredited representative." Ask questions if you do not under-stand what you are being asked to sign.

TWELVE THINGS FOR YOU AND YOUR FAMILY TO REMEMBER IN ANY SITUATION INVOLVING IMMIGRATION.

1 Anything you say can be used against you.

2 You have the right to remain silent.

3 If you wish to remain silent, say it out loud or show your Know Your Rights card.

Get one on page 13!

I AM EXERCISING MY RIGHT TO REMAIN SILENT.

4 Always carry U.S. identification and copies of immigration documents.

5 Never carry false documents or documents from another country.

6 Never lie to officers.

7 You have the right to speak with your attorney.

8 Never run in a raid or if you are approached by officers.

9 Never physically fight back if you are being arrested or detained.

10 You have the right to refuse to sign anything before speaking with your attorney.

11 If you are in police custody or detention, do not discuss your immigration information or criminal history with ANYONE other than your attorney.

12 If you are questioned or in a raid, write down what happened in detail as soon as it is safe to do so. Tell your attorney and your support groups right away.

KNOW YOUR RIGHTS CARD

INSTRUCTIONS ON HOW TO USE YOUR KNOW YOUR RIGHTS CARD

1. Cut out the two copies of the card. Fold them in half.
2. Make sure to fill out both cards with the name of your attorney and your attorney's phone number.
3. Keep both copies of the card with you at all times. If you show immigration officers or the police this card, they make take the card and not return it. This is why it is important to carry two copies of the card at all times.
4. In the event of a raid or interaction with immigration officers or the police, use this card to help you remember and exercise your rights.
5. On the front of this card is a statement that you are exercising your right to remain silent. If you are inter-acting with immigration officers or the police, you should remember that anything you say can be used against you. It is your right to remain silent. To exercise your right to remain silent, show officers a copy of this card or read the statement out loud. You do not need to say the statement word-for-word but you must communicate that you are exercising your right to remain silent.
6. On the back of the card you will find a list of your rights. Read them often. Be prepared.
7. To protect yourself, MEMORIZE the information on the card.

Card (left copy)

I AM EXERCISING MY RIGHT TO REMAIN SILENT.

Please be informed that I am choosing to exercise my right to remain silent. I am also exercising my right to refuse to sign anything until my attorney reviews it. If I am detained, I request to contact my attorney immediately. My attorney's contact information is:

Name _____

Phone _____

I know that...

1. I have rights. I have dignity. I am not alone.
2. I have the right to speak to my attorney.
3. I have the right to refuse to sign anything before my attorney reviews it.
4. Anything I say can be used against me.
5. I have the right to remain silent in ANY situation.
6. I can show officials this card or say out loud that I am remaining silent.

Fold

Card (right copy)

I AM EXERCISING MY RIGHT TO REMAIN SILENT.

Please be informed that I am choosing to exercise my right to remain silent. I am also exercising my right to refuse to sign anything until my attorney reviews it. If I am detained, I request to contact my attorney immediately. My attorney's contact information is:

Name _____

Phone _____

I know that...

1. I have rights. I have dignity. I am not alone.
2. I have the right to speak to my attorney.
3. I have the right to refuse to sign anything before my attorney reviews it.
4. Anything I say can be used against me.
5. I have the right to remain silent in ANY situation.
6. I can show officials this card or say out loud that I am remaining silent.

EMERGENCY PLANNING GUIDE

Emergency plan for:

Find an attorney or accredited representative who will help you in the event of an emergency. Make sure to speak with the attorney or accredited representative. Do not just write down the phone number without making sure the person will be able to help you.

Get screened by an attorney or accredited representative to determine if you are eligible for another immigration status.

Register with your local consulate.

Register and form a relationship with your church, parish or other religious or community center.

Make a family plan about what to do in the event a family member is arrested, detained or goes missing.

- Decide who will be called and in what order.
- In some states, the law requires you to give your name to the police. Find out whether you are required to provide your name in your state. Make a plan about what you will do if you are asked your name. Consider that not giving your name could cause you to be arrested or detained. Not giving your name could make it difficult or impossible for your family to locate you in detention or police custody. Speak to an attorney about what to do in your unique situation.

Make copies of all immigration and other important papers for all members of the family. Keep them in a safe place. Make sure a trusted friend, family member that does not live with you or member of the community knows where you keep these papers or make a set of copies for them to keep. *Important papers:*

- Work authorization
- Copies of identification
- Passports
- Copies of any other immigration papers, including receipt notices for any pending cases and approval notices for family petitions
- Birth certificates (with English translations)
- Marriage certificates (with English translations)
- Social Security cards
- Documents related to criminal arrests or cases
- Name and contact information for attorneys who have represented you in the past

- Other important information such as a list of medications family members take

Decide who will take care of your children in an emergency. Make sure that person has important information about your children, such as medications they need. Speak to an attorney to see if you should sign any legal documents (such as a power of attorney) to make sure your children are cared for in the event of an emergency. Make sure children born in the United States have passports.

Speak to your attorney about signing a power of attorney. A power of attorney will allow someone you trust to take care of decisions involving your finances, children and other needs if you are detained or deported.

Save money for rent, food, medications and other needs if you are detained. Talk to your attorney or employer about signing a document allowing a family member to pick up your paycheck if you are detained.

Ask a relative, friend or member of the community to post bond for you if you are detained. This person must be a U.S. citizen or Lawful Permanent Resident (green card holder). A bond to be released from immigration detention is usually $1,500, but it can be more. In most cases, once your immigration case is over, the bond money will be returned.

Review this guide and your emergency plan with your entire family. MAKE SURE EVERYONE IN YOUR FAMILY KNOWS THEIR RIGHTS. You may want to practice exactly what you will say and do in the event of contact with an officer.

INFORMATION YOU MUST MEMORIZE

The phone number of your attorney (also carry a copy of your attorney's phone number with you at all times).

The phone number of your consulate (also carry a copy of your consulate's phone number with you at all times).

The phone numbers of family members.

Your Alien Registration Number/A# (the number on your immigration documents), if applicable.

Your date of entry into the United States.

Your immigration status when you entered the United States.

Your current immigration status.

Your criminal history – including any arrests, charges, the outcome (guilty or innocent), and dates.

EMERGENCY CONTACT SHEET

Make sure all members of your family have access to this information.

Attorney/accredited representative

    Name: _____

    Phone: _____

Consulate

    Name: _____

    Phone: _____

Religious or community organization

Name: _____

Phone: _____

Other:

Name: _____

Phone: _____

Other:

Name: _____

Phone: _____

Other:

Name: _____

Phone: _____

Detention Centers and Police Stations

Make sure all members of your family have access to this information.

Immigration Court Information System (for information about hearings and court dates): 1-800-898-7180 ICE Detainee Locator system: locator.ice.gov

Local Immigration Detention Center:

Name: _____

Phone: _____

Local Police Station:

Name: _____

Phone: _____

QUESTIONS TO ASK IF A LOVED ONE CALLS YOU FROM DETENTION OR POLICE CUSTODY:

Make sure to record the answers carefully and in as much detail as possible.

- Do you need medical attention?
- What law enforcement agency arrested or detained you?
- Where are you?
- What is the largest city or town near you?
- What papers have you been given and what do the papers say?
- Do you have any court date or hearing scheduled?
- Have you spoken with your attorney/accredited representative?

WORKPLACE CHECKLIST

Review the information in this guide with your co-workers. Make sure that everyone knows their rights. Remember that immigration officers can raid your workplace 1) with a warrant, or 2) with permission from your employer.

If you are a member of a labor union, speak to your union representative about what you can do to protect yourself and other co-workers who are at risk.

If possible, speak with your union representative to come up with an agreement with your employer. An agreement could include:

1. The employer will not permit immigration officers to enter the workplace without a valid warrant.
2. The employer will notify the union if immigration authorities contact the employer.

3. The employer will allow the union to bring immigration attorneys or advocates to the workplace to assist employees with questions and to prepare for an emergency.
4. The employer will not provide the name, address or any immigration information to police or immigration officers, unless it is required by law.
5. The employer will not use computer verification programs to look at employee immigration information.

Make a plan about what to do in the event of a raid. For example, it would be beneficial if everyone agrees to remain silent and not run.

Your employer should be responsible for speaking with officers during a raid. In the event your employer is not present during a raid or if your employer has given permission to the officers to enter, elect a representative(s) to ask officers for identification and review any warrants they present.

Make sure that person knows how to read a warrant and what a warrant requires. Use the information about warrants in this guide to help prepare.

CHAPTER 18

5 WAYS TO CHECK THE STATUS OF YOUR PENDING APPLICATION WITH USCIS

"This is a new nation, based on a mighty continent, of boundless possibilities." - Theodore Roosevelt

After you've filed your petition or application with USCIS, what happens next? It takes time for USCIS to process your case, so it's important to keep track on the status to ensure that your petition or application is processed in a timely manner and to check to see if there are any issues that may cause a delay in the processing of your case.

USCIS receives thousands of petitions and applications every year so processing times vary depending on the type of case you've filed and where you've filed it. You can check the processing times of the field offices, service centers, and National Benefits Center here for Processing Times (egov.uscis.gov).

Some petitioner and applications can take several weeks to be approved and others can take several months to process.

Here are the different ways you can track the status of your case:

Phone
One way to check the status of your pending case is to call USCIS at 1-800-375-5283. You can call them whether or not you have a receipt number. Depending on how busy they are, you can be placed on hold anywhere from two minutes to two hours.

Online at the USCIS Website
A simple way to check the status of your pending case is to go to the USCIS website: USCIS Check Status. You will need your 13-character receipt number (ex. WAC-01-234-56789) in order to check online.

Email/Text/Phone App
You can also sign up for automatic updates and have them sent to your email by creating an account with USCIS and providing your email address: USCIS Sign-up for Case Updates. If you prefer to have updates on your case sent to your phone, after you've created an account, you can provide your phone number to receive a text message notifying you when a case status update has occurred. You will need your receipt number for both these options. There are also various types of phone apps you can use as well to track the status of your case such as USCIS Case Status Notifier (Android), Case Status Lite (Apple and Android), USCIS Helper (Apple), and USCIS Checker (Apple, Android, and Windows).

Mail
You can also request a case status update by mail if you've filed

your petition or application through a local USCIS Field Office. In your letter, you'll need to provide your personal information such as your full name, birth date, alien number (if applicable), the date and place your petition or application was filed, and your receipt number (if you've received one). You should also include a copy of your receipt notice if you have it.

In Person

If you wish to find out the status of your case in person, you can schedule an InfoPass appointment (immigration appointment scheduler) with your local office and speak with an immigration officer. You can schedule an InfoPass appointment here: https://www.uscis.gov/outreach/uscis-infopass-appointment-scheduler

So, what's the best way to keep updated on your case status? Most people prefer to have updates sent to their email or phone so that they don't have to constantly go to the USCIS website to check.

(Source: Jackie Tang. Bridge US 2014)

If you have any questions about checking the status of your USCIS Application feel free to schedule some time to talk with our team at Be Informed Immigrant. (Email: contact@beinformedimmigrant.com)

CHAPTER 19

FREQUENTLY ASKED MARRIAGE-BASED GREEN CARD INTERVIEW QUESTIONS

"The greatest nations are defined by how they treat their weakest inhabitants." – Jorge Ramos

Typically, Marriage-Based Adjustment of Status applications require both the applicant and the spouse to be present for an interview before the case can be approved. For many applicants, the thought of being interviewed by an immigration officer can be stressful and overwhelming. However, applicants who are well-prepared should not worry! The Green Card interview is more of a formality and typically lasts no longer than thirty minutes. It is often compared to a job interview.

Below we will list some sample interview questions you may be asked during your marriage-based green card interview. Please remember that there is no guarantee the officer will ask you any or all of these questions. This is meant to be used as a tool to help familiarize applicants with the types of questions that may be asked.

Relationship Development:
- Where did you meet?
- Where did you go on your first date?

- Were you introduced to each other's friends?
- When did you realize you loved your spouse?
- Who proposed to whom?
- How did they propose?

The Wedding:
- Where did you get married?
- How many people attended?
- What did your spouse wear?
- Did you have a reception or any type of celebration?
- Was there any type of entertainment?
- Who were the bridesmaids/groomsmen?
- What was the color scheme?
- What flavor was the wedding cake?
- Did you go on a honeymoon? If so, where?

Daily Life:
- Who gets up first?
- How many alarms do you set?
- Who sleeps on what side of the bed?
- What do you each eat for breakfast?
- Who is your spouse's employer?
- What time do you each arrive home from work?
- Who does the dishes?
- What day is your garbage picked up?
- Who takes care of the finances?
- Do you have any pets? Who takes care of it?
- Where do you keep the spare toilet paper?

Nighttime Routines:
- What size is your bed?

- How many windows are in your bedroom?
- Do you have a television in your bedroom?
- What color is your comforter?
- What kind of toothpaste do you use?
- Does your spouse read or watch television before bed?
- What kind of pajamas does your spouse wear?

The Home:
- Do you live in a home or an apartment?
- How much is your mortgage or rent?
- Do you have a garage? Who parks in it?
- What color is your sofa?
- Where do house guests sleep?
- What type of window coverings do you have in your living room?
- How many bathrooms are in your house?
- Do you leave any lights on when you leave the house?
- Do you use the front, side or back door?

The Cooking:
- How many times a week would you say you order take out?
- What is your favorite place to order pizza?
- What restaurant do you frequent as a couple?
- Who does most of the cooking?
- Who typically goes grocery shopping?
- Where do you get your groceries?
- What is your spouse's favorite food?
- What color is your kitchen painted?
- Do you have a barbecue or grill?
- Is your stove gas or electric?

Family:

- Have you met each other's families?
- How often do you see each other's families?
- When was the last time you saw them?
- How do you typically celebrate holidays? For example, do you spend Thanksgiving with one family and Christmas with another?
- On holidays, do you buy each other's family members gifts?
- How many brothers and sisters does your spouse have? What are their names?
- Does your spouse have any nieces or nephews?

Technology:

- What television service do you use?
- What type of cell phone does your spouse have?
- Do you have a television show you like to watch together?
- How many computers are in the house?
- What is your Wifi password?
- What kind of car does your spouse drive?
- Do they listen to the radio in the car? What station?

Celebrations:

- When is your spouse's birthday?
- When is your anniversary?
- What did your spouse get you for your last birthday?
- Do you celebrate any religious holidays or regularly attend church?
- What's your spouse's favorite holiday?
- Have you ever dressed up as a couple for Halloween?
- What did you do last New Year's Eve?
- What movie did you last see together?

(Source: Berardi Immigration Law 2015)

For more tips on what to expect at your Adjustment of Status interview, please visit our website (www.Beinformedimmigrant.com)

If you are interested in applying for a Green Card or have questions regarding the Green Card interview process, please contact our office today to schedule a consultation with one of our referral attorneys.

CHAPTER 20

HOW TO AVOID MISTAKES IN USCIS FORMS

"People come here penniless but not cultureless. They bring us gifts. We can synthesize the best of our traditions with the best of theirs. We can teach and learn from each other to produce a better America." – Mary Pipher

Here are some of the worst mistake's immigrants make applying for legal papers:

U.S. immigration applications can be complex and cumbersome, so it's always better to work with a licensed immigration attorney. But their legal services can be very expensive, and many immigrants opt to go through the process alone.

However, mistakes are common when filing immigration forms, and the applications can therefore be delayed or denied by the U.S. Citizenship and Immigration Services (USCIS).

These are some of the worst mistakes when it comes to filling paperwork that should be avoided at all costs, according to USCIS:

- Failure to sign a document
  Without a signature, the document is automatically rejected and returned.

- Using outdated forms
  USCIS recommends downloading forms directly from its website, filling in the information requested electronically and then printing them before sending them to its offices.

- Leaving parts of the questionnaire blank
  All forms must be completely filled in.

- Using colored ink or illegible writing
  The forms must be filled in with black ink and in clearly legible lettering inside the spaces provided.

- Don't use highlighters or correction liquids
  USCIS scanners can't easily read text that has been highlighted, crossed out or written over correction fluid or tape.

- Submitting forms with corrections
  USCIS recommends starting over with a new form instead of trying to correct a mistake.

- Failure to repeat vital information
  Regardless of how many forms are being submitted, each one must carry the full name of the applicant, date of birth and Alien number (A-number) if available.

- Paying the wrong fee
  Problems with benefit petition fees, specifically sending incorrect payments, are a constant reason for denying immigration petitions.

USCIS launched an online tool in January this year to calculate the correct fees for the forms being submitted.

"USCIS is focused on offering support to those applying for immigration benefits. Everything from the tips on our website to our online tools such as the fee calculator, are meant to make the process as easy as possible," said Ana Santiago, the agency's spokesperson for South Florida.

PREPARING THE PACKET

Once the forms have been filled in, applicants can make mistakes putting together all the documents and supporting materials that are sent with the main petition.

USCIS pointed to these key mistakes:

- Binding the documents
  USCIS employees need to be able to easily separate the documents, so avoid folders and binders.

- Stapling the documents
  The agency recommends using paper clips instead of heavy-duty staples. If the package is too thick, it's preferable to punch two holes on the top of the material.

- Sticky labels
  It's OK to use them but put them at the bottom of the page, not the sides.

- Original documents
  Do not submit original documents. Submit photocopies, unless originals are specifically requested.

- Submitting large files
  It's preferable to avoid oversized files, unless absolutely necessary.

- Mixing documents from different cases
  If the applicant is submitting two cases in the same envelope, it's important to separate them clearly with either a rubber band or butterfly clips.

- Sending the package to the wrong location
  USCIS may reject and return applications or petitions that are improperly filed.

(Source: DANIEL SHOER ROTH. Miami Herald 2019)

PART FIVE

DON'T WAIT TOO LONG TO END UP BECOMING A STATISTIC

CHAPTER 21

WHAT TO DO IF AN IMMIGRATION OR BORDER PATROL OFFICER CONFRONTS YOU

"He doesn't like my name . . . Of course we couldn't all come over on the Mayflower . . . But I got here as soon as I could, and I never wanted to go back, because to me it is a great privilege to be an American citizen." – Anton Cermak

Anti-immigrant rhetoric, along with policy moves by the Trump administration, have revived fears over immigration raids and mass deportations in the United States. Recently, U.S. Immigration and Customs Enforcement (ICE) agents raided dozens of 7-Eleven stores nationwide on suspicion of hiring undocumented immigrants.

And in South Florida, U.S. Border Patrol agents stopped a Greyhound bus en route to Orlando and demanded citizenship documentation, detaining a Jamaican citizen.

For the record: under federal statutes, immigration officials do have the authority to "board and search for aliens in any vessel within the territorial waters of the United States and any rail car, aircraft, conveyance, or vehicle" within 100 miles of a land or sea border. In Florida, that means the entire state.

Some advocates disagree with this interpretation and contend that actions such as boarding buses solely traveling in the interior of the state may violate the Fourth Amendment.

However, should you find yourself in a situation like this, whether in public spaces, places of employment or private homes, all residents – including legal and undocumented immigrants – can exercise basic constitutional rights to respond to authorities.

"These enshrined rights are applicable to all people regardless of their immigration status and are a muscle that people should use," says Adonia Simpson, director of the Family Defense program of Americans for Immigration Justice, based in Miami. However, the lawyer emphasizes, that "does not guarantee that the rights are not violated; that immigrants are not detained."

These include the right to remain silent, the right to deny permission to a search of your person, vehicle or home, and the right to request a lawyer. What should you do when the authorities ask for your papers?

Here are some tips:

KEEP SILENT

Everyone has the right to remain silent by refusing to answer questions. It is advisable to give your name and the date of birth, so that your relatives can easily find you. But if you wish to exercise this right, say these words: "I exercise my right to remain silent."

DO NOT LIE OR SIGN

You do not have to answer questions about place of birth or how you entered the country, or give explanations or excuses. But never claim to be a U.S. citizen if you aren't one, or give false identification documents. Do not sign papers without legal advice either, as you may be signing your own deportation orders, or reveal your immigration status to anyone other than your lawyer.

U.S. BORN CITIZENS

If a U.S. citizen is asked for proof of citizenship, he or she can choose not to answer, but there is a risk of being detained.

The Department of Homeland Security has ways to verify if someone is a U.S. citizen, however, there have been occasions where U.S. citizens have been detained or deported. Experts recommend that U.S. citizens know how to access some way of proof of citizenship like a passport, passport card, birth certificate, certificate of naturalization or certification of citizenship.

NATURALIZED IMMIGRANTS

Naturalized immigrants can inform agents that they are citizens of the United States. In theory, a citizen should not be detained by ICE agents, but if the person can't immediately corroborate their citizenship status by presenting a passport, voter's card, naturalization certificate or other evidence, then he or she can be taken to a detention center.

PERMANENT RESIDENTS

Experts recommend that permanent residents keep their immigration documents with them, such as their permanent residence card or green card. In the case of foreigners with non-immigrant visas, make sure to have handy an I-94 card, employment authorization or other valid document that proves registration with Citizenship and Immigration Services (USCIS). If you do not have them, stay calm and remain silent.

MEMORIZE IDENTIFICATION NUMBERS
This includes the foreign A # registration number with a nine-digit series and, if arrested, the prison identification number or name. Also memorize the telephone number of a close relative, any medications you take and your current immigration status, as well as criminal records, if any.

CONSULT WITH A LAWYER
Before answering any questions, you can immediately ask for a lawyer. You are also entitled to a local call and to contact the consulate of your home country. However, the United States does not guarantee a free lawyer in immigration processes. And notaries are not lawyers.

PLAN OF ACTION WITH FAMILY
If you are detained, it is preferable to have an action plan outlined, with an authorized emergency contact to pick up your children at school and make medical and legal decisions on their behalf. Keep in a secure place proof of your physical presence in the United States, such as rental agreements, income statements and financial information.

DENY HOME ENTRY
If ICE agents arrive at your home, you do not have to open the door unless they file a search warrant or arrest warrant.

Ask them to pass the order under the door and verify that it is signed by a judge. A deportation/removal order (ICE warrant) does not authorize entry without your permission. If you want to deny their entry, you can say: "I do not give you permission to enter. I will remain silent until I speak to an attorney. "

Sources: National Immigrant Justice Center, Florida Immigrant Coalition, Americans for Immigrant Justice, and the American Civil Liberties Union. For more information visit the websites of these organizations.

(Source: DANIEL SHOER ROTH. Miami Herald 2018)

CHAPTER 22

5 WAYS TO LOSE PERMANENT RESIDENT STATUS

"Everywhere immigrants have enriched and strengthened the fabric of American life." – John F. Kennedy

As the name suggests, permanent resident status is generally constant. It's granted to people who intend to live in the United States for the foreseeable future. Permanent residents, also known as green card holders, have the privilege of living and working in the United States permanently. However, there are ways to lose permanent resident status. Certain actions can trigger removal (deportation) proceedings and the potential loss of this coveted immigration status.

The article discusses the major ways that one can lose permanent resident status, but it isn't an exhaustive list. Only a lawful permanent resident who naturalizes as a U.S. citizen is safe from most of these grounds of removal.

1. Living Outside the United States

Generally, spending more than twelve months outside the United States will result in a loss of permanent resident status. In fact, shorter absences can trigger abandonment if upon re-entry the Customs and Border Protection (CBP) officer determines that you intended to live outside the United States. For example, failing to file income taxes with the IRS while living outside the U.S. can trigger removal.

Each year many people unintentionally abandon their green card status when they move back to their home country. They may need to take care of a sick family member, attend school or even tend to their own medical needs. Without the right preparation and planning, it leads to the most common way to lose permanent resident status.

Prevention

There are exceptions. Permanent residents who obtain a re-entry permit prior to departure can generally extend their absence up to twenty four months. Additionally, U.S. government personnel (military and direct-hire civil service employees), their spouses and minor children who hold permanent resident status may remain outside of the United States for the duration of an official overseas assignment plus four months without losing their resident status.

Re-acquiring a Visa

A former immigrant who has lost permanent resident status and wants to return to the United States as an immigrant must obtain a new immigrant visa. In most cases, this means that the intending immigrant must re-apply. A U.S. relative (spouse, parent, offspring or sibling) may file an I-130 immigrant petition and the intending immigrant can apply through consular processing once the visa petition is approved and a visa is immediately available.

In some cases, the former permanent resident may apply for

a returning resident visa. An application for returning resident status requires evidence of the applicant's continuing, unbroken ties to the United States, that the stay outside the United States was truly beyond the applicant's control and that the intent of the applicant was to always return to the United States. Evidence may consist of continuous compliance with U.S. tax law, ownership of property and assets in the United States and maintenance of U.S. licenses and memberships. Having U.S. relatives, attending school overseas or stating an intent to return is generally insufficient. It's best to seek the assistance of an immigration attorney when requesting a returning resident visa.

2. Voluntary Surrender of Green Card

If you have ever filed Form I-407, you have voluntarily abandoned your status as a lawful permanent resident of the United States. Each year several thousand people file Form I-407, Record of Abandonment of Lawful Permanent Resident Status.

The most common reason people file Form I-407 is to escape the obligation of paying U.S. taxes. However, anybody that wishes to do this should consult with an immigration attorney and tax professional that can advise them on the long-term consequences of their actions. There are other former U.S. immigrants that simply decide they want to leave the United States permanently.

In some cases, CBP officers may ask certain individuals to sign Form I-407. If you've been living outside the United States (as discussed in the previous section) and the CBP officer believes you have abandoned your U.S. residence, you generally have the right to defend yourself in removal proceedings. The officer may ask you to sign Form I-407 so that you give up this opportunity to defend yourself and voluntarily deport yourself. If your intention is to continue your permanent residence, do not sign I-407 and contact an immigration attorney.

3. Fraud and Willful Misrepresentation

A fraud is generally committed when an individual lies to obtain immigration benefits of some kind. However, any assertion or representation of facts that is not completely truthful can create significant immigration problems and potentially result in the loss of permanent resident status.

Fraud can occur when preparing an application, submitting evidence, interviews and any exchange of information with immigration officials. It can occur in connection with immigration benefits other than permanent residence. For example, extensions of nonimmigrant stay, change of status, employment authorization and parole are all immigration benefits that USCIS evaluates for potential fraud.

Two of the more common ways to lose permanent resident status include marriage fraud and visa fraud.

Marriage Fraud

Marriage has been a long-time target of fraud. Since marriage to a U.S. citizen is one of the fastest paths to a green card, it's often used as a vehicle to fraudulently obtain permanent residence. Marriage fraud comes in many different forms. USCIS has identified the following types of marriage fraud:

A U.S. citizen is paid to marry a foreign national.

A U.S. citizen marries a foreign national as a favor.

A foreign national defrauds a U.S. citizen who believes that their marriage is legitimate.

Mail-order marriages (where either the U.S. citizen or the foreign national knows that the marriage is fraudulent).

Visa Lottery Fraudulent Marriages

Nonimmigrant Visa Fraud

Most foreign nationals applying for a U.S. nonimmigrant visa are required to demonstrate that they plan to return home when they are done with their intended program or activity. This standard, known as nonimmigrant intent, requires the individual to have a residence abroad that he or she has no intention of abandoning.

The U.S. Department of State uses a 90-day rule to evaluate cases in which the nonimmigrant attempts to change status or adjust status to permanent resident. The 90-day rule is a guideline of sorts that there's a presumption of fraud if a person violates his or her nonimmigrant status or engages in conduct inconsistent with that status within 90 days of entry. For example, entering the United States on a B2 visa for the purposes of getting married and filing Form I-485 to adjust status would be a violation of the visa terms.

4. Criminal Convictions

Not all criminal convictions will cause an individual to lose permanent resident status. There are certain types of criminal offenses (typically violent crimes) that are more likely to put a permanent resident in removal proceedings.

It's impossible to list a precise list of crimes that will result in deportation. Only an experienced immigration attorney can analyze a specific situation and provide an opinion. Very generally, a person may be removed from the United States if he or she:

Is convicted of a crime involving moral turpitude that was committed within five years after the date of U.S. admission (or ten years if the person received a green card as a criminal informant) and is punishable by a sentence of at least one year.

Has been convicted of two or more crimes involving moral turpitude at any time after U.S. admission, where the two crimes did not arise out of a single scheme of misconduct.

Has been convicted of an aggravated felony at any time after U.S. admission.

Again, this is not a complete list. Even renewing a green card after an arrest can be problematic for certain individuals. Contact an immigration lawyer to discuss your specific case.

If immigration officials believe that a permanent resident is deportable, the individual will generally not be removed immediately. In most cases, the green card holder will have a right to defend himself in immigration court. However, an individual with an outstanding order of removal could be deported more swiftly.

5. Failing to Remove Conditions on Residence
Conditional residents who fail to remove the conditions on

residence are generally removable upon the expiration of their two-year green cards.

Certain foreign national investors or spouses who obtained residence through marriage may have received a two-year conditional green card. In order to remain a permanent resident, the conditional permanent resident must file a petition to remove the condition during the 90 days before the card expires. The conditional card cannot be renewed.

To remove the conditions on a green card based on marriage, you must file Form I-751, Petition to Remove the Conditions of Residence.

To remove conditions on a green card for entrepreneurs, you must file Form I-829, Petition by Entrepreneur to Remove Conditions.

Generally, the foreign national may be put into removal proceedings if the petition is not filed by the expiration date. If the issue is left unaddressed, the foreign national will lose permanent resident status.

Citizenship is the Right Way to Lose Permanent Resident Status
Permanent residents who choose to naturalize as U.S. citizens will also lose permanent resident status in the process. U.S. citizens are protected from grounds of deportability. In other words, criminal convictions that would result in deportation for a permanent resident do not apply to a U.S. citizen. Generally, the only way immigration officials can remove a U.S. citizen is if he or she used fraud to obtain a green card or citizenship.

Many permanent residents who have resided in the United States for at least five years are now eligible to file Form N-400, Application for Naturalization.

(Source: Citizen Path 2018)

If you need to learn more about the naturalization process and citizenship requirements, reach out to us for more information or visit our website: www.beinformedimmigrant.com

CHAPTER 23

WHEN TRAVELING ABROAD AFFECT CITIZENSHIP ELIGIBILITY

"We are a nation of immigrants. We are the children and grandchildren and great-grandchildren of the ones who wanted a better life, the driven ones, the ones who woke up at night hearing that voice telling them that life in that place called America could be better." – Mitt Romney

When applying for U.S. citizenship via naturalization, English and civics tests get much of the attention. But permanent residents often do not understand how travel abroad can affect their eligibility for naturalization.

Two related but separate requirements, continuous residence and physical presence, must be satisfied for one to be eligible to file Form N-400, Application for Naturalization. Excessive travel abroad can adversely affect eligibility. Excessive travel can include one long trip or the accumulation of several trips over the period that precedes your admission as a U.S. citizen.

Continuous Residence
Continuous residence means that the applicant has maintained residence within the United States for a specified period of time. An applicant must have continuous residence in the United

States as a lawful permanent resident for at least five years immediately preceding the date of filing N-400, Application for Naturalization. The continuous residence requirement is adjusted to three years for an applicant's filing as a permanent resident married to a U.S. citizen, and the requirement may be waived completely for applications submitted on the basis of military service for example.

The purpose of the continuous residence requirement is to establish the applicant's genuine intent to be an American citizen and not just take advantage of the benefits of U.S. citizenship. USCIS wants to know that the applicant truly wants to become a citizen. The continuous residence requirement helps the applicant demonstrate that he or she has begun to integrate with American community and intends to stay in the U.S. long term. So how long can one be absent from the United States?

Disrupting the Continuous Residence Requirement

In general, the following guidelines apply for permanent residents who are traveling abroad:

A trip abroad that is less than six months will not disrupt continuous residence.

A trip abroad of six to twelve months will likely disrupt continuous residence.

A trip abroad twelve months or longer will disrupt continuous residence.

USCIS officers are also well aware of the games some people

play. They will examine all of the trips taken during the five years that precedes the filing of the application. USCIS will notice if the applicant has taken multiple trips which appear calculated to take less than six months. (For example, the applicant travels abroad for five months and fifteen days, returns to the U.S. for ten days, then leaves again for another five months.) The USCIS officer may consider the two separate trips as one long trip of more than ten months.

Physical Presence
Physical presence means that the applicant has been physically present within the United States for a specified period of time. A permanent resident must have thirty months of physical presence in the United States over the five years immediately preceding the date of filing N-400, Application for Naturalization. The physical presence requirement is reduced to eighteen months for permanent residents married to a U.S. citizen (over a three-year period). And again the requirement may be waived for certain applicants who have served the U.S. government.

Unlike continuous residence, physical presence is a cumulative requirement. When calculating physical presence, the permanent resident must combine each day that he or she was outside the United States. If a permanent resident that spends more time abroad than in the United States, it raises concerns that the U.S. may not be his or her true home.

Calculate Continuous Residence & Physical Presence
An N-400 applicant can determine time as a permanent resident by reviewing his or her green card. The date that permanent

residence status began can be found on the green card next to "Resident Since." Calculate this manually.

Determine Continuous Residence for US Citizenship

Note: If you came here as a refugee, your permanent residence date will be backdated to the day you arrived in the United States. If you were initially in asylum status, it will be backdated one year.

USCIS will count the day that an applicant departs from the United States and the day he or she returns as days of physical presence within the United States for naturalization purposes.

Travel as a Permanent Resident

Lawful permanent residents are allowed to travel abroad freely and re-enter the United States with a valid green card. But extensive travel may affect permanent resident status as well as eligibility for U.S. citizenship.

As a rule, permanent residents should not travel outside the United States for periods of six months or more. When a permanent resident spends significant time outside the United States, it may give rise to the notion that he/she has abandoned his/her permanent resident status.

Travel Under Six Months

A permanent resident may generally leave the United States and re-enter less than six months later without any issues. To re-enter he or she must provide valid proof of permanent resident status. For most people a valid permanent resident card (green card) that has not expired can be used for re-entry. Use Form I-90, Application to Replace Permanent Resident

Card, to renew a green card that will expire in six months or less.

Travel Longer Than Six Months But Less Than a Year

If an applicant is absent from the United States for a period of more than six months, but less than one year, there will be a presumption that he or she has disrupted continuous resident. This includes any absence that takes place prior to filing the naturalization application or between filing and the applicant's admission to citizenship. The applicant will have to demonstrate proof of residence. In other words, the person will have to show that he/she did not abandon residence in the U.S. and that the U.S. is the primary place of residence. Although many applicants have done this on their own, it is recommended that you seek the support and advice of an immigration attorney that can help you document your case. Examples of evidence may include, but are not limited to the applicant:

Did not terminate his or her employment in the United States or obtain employment while abroad.

Immediate family remained in the United States.

Retained full access to his or her United States residence.

Travel Longer Than One Year

An absence from the United States for a period of one year or more during the period for which continuous residence is required will break the continuous residence requirement. Again, the applicable period includes time prior to and after filing the naturalization application.

What's more, if a permanent resident stays outside the U.S. for one year or longer without securing a reentry permit, the government may try to revoke the person's permanent residence.

Re-entry Permit for Travel Before Naturalization

A naturalization applicant who is required to establish continuous residence for at least five years and whose application for naturalization is denied due to an absence of one year or longer, may apply for naturalization four years and one day after returning to the United States to resume permanent residence. (An applicant who is subject to the three-year continuous residence requirement may apply two years and one day after returning to the United States to resume permanent residence.)

Most attorneys prefer that their clients do not travel abroad once the applicant has filed Form N-400. However, it is possible. If you would like to travel outside the United States during the naturalization process or if you plan to travel abroad for a period of six months or more, please speak to an experienced immigration attorney that can explain the ramifications.

Travel Abroad After Filing Form N-400

Many naturalization applicants want to know if it's permissible to travel abroad after filing Form N-400, Application for Naturalization. The simple answer is "yes," but there are several considerations. First, you continue to be a permanent resident and have the right to travel outside the United States, even after filing Form N-400. But your absence from the U.S. still has the potential to interfere with your eligibility and the application process.

Continuous Residence

The continuous residence requirement is still in effect. You must have resided continuously in the United States after your permanent residence admission for at least five years prior to filing the naturalization application and up to the time of naturalization. (For an applicant applying on the basis of three years of permanent residence while married to a U.S. citizen, the same is true. The continuous residence requirement counts up to the time of naturalization.) Therefore, the trip should be short and certainly less than six months in duration.

USCIS Appointments

Another consideration when traveling abroad after filing Form N-400 is the obligation to attend mandatory USCIS appointments. For most candidates, there will be three key appointments: the biometrics appointment, the naturalization interview, and the oath ceremony. While each can be rescheduled, you should make every attempt to attend the appointment as scheduled. Missing an appointment and failure to address the absence can lead to a denial of your application. We can provide an approximate N-400 time-line that outlines the steps after filing Form N-400. However, these appointments will be scheduled by USCIS and can deviate from the estimated time-line.

Exceptions to Continuous Residence and Physical Presence Requirements

There are special provisions in the law that exempt members of the U.S. armed forces, certain business travelers, religious workers, government employees, and researchers for a U.S. research agency, from the continuous residence requirement. This allows certain individuals to maintain eligibility for U.S.

citizenship despite travel abroad for long periods.

Such applicants must file a Form N-470, Application to Preserve Residence for Naturalization Purposes. The following criteria must be met to qualify for Form N-470:

The applicant must have been physically present in the United States as a lawful permanent resident for an uninterrupted period of at least one year prior to working abroad.

The application may be filed either before or after the applicant's employment begins, but before the applicant has been abroad for a continuous period of one year.

In addition, the applicant must have been:

Employed with or under contract with the U.S. Government or an American institution of research recognized as such by the Attorney General;

Employed by an American firm or corporation engaged in the development of U.S. foreign trade and commerce, or a subsidiary thereof if more than fifty percent of its stock is owned by an American firm or corporation; or

Employed by a public international organization of which the United States is a member by a treaty or statute and by which the applicant was not employed until after becoming a lawful permanent resident.

If you believe that you may meet these criteria, contact an experienced immigration attorney to discuss your options.

(Source: Citizen Path 2018)

CHAPTER 24

IMMIGRANTS FACING DEPORTATION DON'T ALWAYS HAVE TO LEAVE THE U.S.

"The land (America) flourished because it was fed from so many sources – because it was nourished by so many cultures and traditions and peoples." – Lyndon B. Johnson

If you know an immigrant facing deportation or you are one, you have rights.

Here's what you can do.

The restrictive immigration policies proposed and implemented by the Trump administration, including expanding the list of reasons for which immigrants can be summoned to appear before immigration judges to start deportation procedures, have increased immigrants' fears of being removed from the United States.

Immigrants may be detained and deported by the U.S. Immigration and Customs Enforcement (ICE) agency if they entered the country illegally, participated in criminal acts, violated the terms of the visas or pose a threat to public safety.

If immigrants facing deportation orders are held in a detention center, they have few options to avoid removal. But if they have been placed under an order of supervision as part of their removal proceedings, there are ways to appeal, seek other legal avenues to resolve the case or halt the deportation temporarily.

What should a person do if he or she is facing deportation proceedings? Depending on an individual's particular situation, these tips may help.

APPLY FOR A STAY OF DEPORTATION OR REMOVAL
Foreign nationals are able to appeal certain deportation rulings, with legal advice from attorneys licensed to practice Immigration law in the U.S. In the process, they can apply for a stay of deportation or removal.

To apply, they must submit Form I-246 in person at an ICE Enforcement and Removal Operations (ERO) field office and pay a $155 application fee. Applicants must also submit their valid original passports, or copies of passports with a copy of a birth certificate or other original ID document. Always confirm current fees from USCIS website: www.uscis.gov.

The applications must be accompanied by evidence supporting the reasons why they are requesting a stay, such as medical documentation, police reports or sentencing documents.

ERO field offices are listed in this ICE link. https://www.ice.gov/contact/ero

EXPLORE IF YOU ARE ABLE TO GET A GREEN CARD
Adjusting a status to get a green card may void a deportation

order, if the immigrant in fact qualifies to become a lawful permanent resident. There are two ways to qualify:

- **Family petition**

There are two categories of family relationships: immediate relatives, and other family members described by the government as "preferences immigrants." They must make the petition using Form I-130.

- **Asylum**

Immigrants facing deportation may seek asylum if they prove credible fear of persecution or torture in their country, or fear persecution if they are returned, because of their race, religion, nationality, political opinion or membership in a social group. The application can be submitted using Form I-589.

FILE A CIVIL RIGHTS COMPLAINT WITH HOMELAND SECURITY

Immigrants who believe their civil rights were violated while in immigration detention or as a subject of immigration enforcement may file complaints with the Department of Homeland Security's Office for Civil Rights and Civil Liberties (CRCL).

Every person in the United States has constitutional rights, regardless of their immigration status. These include the right to remain silent, the right to deny permission to a search of your person, vehicle or home, and the right to request a lawyer.

You can file a civil rights complaint in this DHS link. https://www.dhs.gov/how-do-i/file-civil-rights-complaint

LEAVE THE U.S. VOLUNTARILY

If none of these options are feasible, an immigrant who's not in ICE detention can be granted by an immigration judge the permission of voluntary departure, which authorizes him or her to remain in the U.S. until a specific date.

Once in their home country, they must go in person to the U.S. Embassy or consulate to verify their voluntary departure and report it to DHS completing Form I-210 or G-146. They need to submit a copy of their passport and their departure airline boarding pass.

This option has advantages because it leaves no record of a deportation and leaves open the possibility of returning later to the United States with a legal entry visa since it does not lead to a period of inadmissibility.

LOCATING PERSONS DETAINED BY ICE

Immigrants held in an ICE detention facility may be located using the agency's Online Detainee Locator System. Friends, relatives and attorneys can also telephone any ERO field office.

The online searches can be done in two ways:

- **A-Number**

That's the nine-digit number, starting with the letter A, assigned to each foreigner during any immigration procedure. People must also select the detainee's country of birth.

- **Biographical information**

Requires the name and surname of the immigrant detained as well as the detainee's country and date of birth.

(Source: DANIEL SHOER ROTH. Miami Herald 2019)

CONCLUSION

"I had always hoped that this land might become a safe and agreeable asylum to the virtuous and persecuted part of mankind, to whatever nation they might belong."
– George Washington

Knowledge + action = power

This is what I tell my students and clients, we know that, knowledge gives you power, but it only gives potential power. But when you act on that knowledge by taking action, then your knowledge becomes real power. And the benefits that flow from that power positively impacts more than one person.

Citizenship/Naturalization

You came to the United States many years ago through a family or employment visa or as a refugee or asylee. You worked hard and eventually obtained lawful permanent resident status. You have waited the required time period and are ready to move ahead towards becoming a full U.S. citizen. If that is the choice you have made, most of the attorneys that I talk to, give two pieces of advice:

(1) Don't wait any longer. They also say that if you don't think you can do it alone. (2) Don't go it alone.

Lady Liberty Right Foot

Have you ever noticed that Lady Liberty has a raised foot, that she's in the middle of walking? Dave Eggers writes, "Liberty and freedom from oppression are not things you get or you are granted by standing around like some kind of statue. No! These are things that require action. Courage. And unwillingness to rest."

Get serious

You cannot keep waiting for some imagined signs before you force yourself to get serious. If you have been waiting for one, perhaps you ought to consider this material that I share with you to be your sign. You must identify your current opportunities and take advantage of them.

While the reality may seem stark, our faith gives us reason to hope and work towards a better future for ourselves and our families. And for our sisters and brothers.

You can do it! You can change your life and your future and the future of your loved ones. And you can do it right away by simply developing a new sense of urgency that is created as a result of a new way of thinking.

Changing the way you think about this subject (hopefully I have supplied enough knowledge to effect that change) can change the way you feel about it and hence enable you to take the right cause of action at any given opportunity.

To your success,

Joe K. Mungai, LMSW

DISCLAIMER

Be Informed Immigrant is a private company that provides referral services and self-directed immigration services at your direction. Self-help might not be permitted in all states and the information provided in this book does not constitute legal advice but general information on issues commonly encountered in immigration field. The information shared does not establish a practitioner or legal relationship. Be informed immigrant is not a law firm and is not a substitute for an attorney or law firm. If you need legal advice, please contact a lawyer directly or reach out to us and we will connect you with one.

Join our Be Informed Immigrant community group.

You are also invited to join the larger immigrant community and learn from their experiences. You can join by visiting our website (www.beinformedimmigrant.com) or through our Facebook community

Facebook: https://fb.me/aninformedimmigrant

Tweeter: https://twitter.com/BeImmigrant

If we can be of further help to you reach out to us with questions and feedback:

Email address: contact@beinformedimmigrant.com

Mailing address:
In U.S. use P.O. Box 5204 Coralville IA 52241 USA. In Kenya use P.O. Box 2748-01000, Thika

ABOUT THE AUTHOR

Joe K. Mungai is the Founder and Executive Director of Be Informed Immigrant, an organization that provides advocacy and education to immigrants and members of the refugee community. This is in addition to referral services for all types of legal issues and a myriad of other support involving immigrants. Be Informed Immigrant also shares helpful content on various immigration topics that are prepared by the attorneys on its referral list.

As an ordained minister and a licensed social worker, and having navigated the immigration system himself, Joe has a unique perspective and insights that benefit every person he supports.

He received his BA degree in social work, and a Master's Degree also in social work, all from the University of Iowa.

He conducts workshops and seminars on topics related to empowering immigrants and has written three upcoming books about: How to avoid detention, deportation and family separation. Overcoming your past (limiting mindsets) and High achievers thinking habits among others.

His other books include *BROKEN JUSTICE: WHEN LAWLESS GANGS CAPTURE THE STATE,* and *LIFE AFTER LOSS: YOU CAN HEAL YOUR WOUNDED HEART.*

As a transformational practitioner, Joe's main area of interest has been to empower immigrants through education and connecting them with vital services, resources and support that improves not only their legal status but their quality of life as well.

www.ingramcontent.com/pod-product-compliance
Lightning Source LLC
Chambersburg PA
CBHW071854020426
42331CB00010B/2511